180 Not Out

**A pictorial history of cricket in
Halifax, Huddersfield, Dewsbury and District**

Volume 1: Calderdale

Compiled by Peter Davies & Rob Light

Published by Sigma Books, March 2006

First published in 2006 by:
Sigma Books, White Hollow, High Street,
East Ilsley, Newbury, Berks RG20 7LE

ISBN 0-905291-04-3

Printed and bound by:
Ridgeway Press, Pangbourne, Berks RG8 7JW

Front cover illustration: Willie Kershaw, Greetland CC

Contents

This series of books is called '180 Not Out' on account of the fact that the first cricket club to be established in our area of research was Lascelles Hall, Huddersfield, in 1825. And it was exactly 180 years on - 2005 - when our Project came to fruition.

**It is more than a game,
this cricket, it somehow
holds a mirror up
to English society.**

Neville Cardus

Dedication

This book, and the series as a whole, is dedicated to the wonderful people who work day and night to keep cricket alive in local communities, and to all those generous cricket folk who have helped us with our research.

Acknowledgements

We have many people to thank for their help in the preparation of this book. First, the officials of the cricket clubs and cricket leagues in the area, who have supported our work enthusiastically and passed on valuable items and images for our archive. Second, the many individuals who have supplied us with historical information and/or images – we have really appreciated this.

In terms of our colleagues, we would like to say a massive thank you to Lee Booth, Sue Brant, Andrew Hardcastle, Alex Heywood, Brian Heywood and Tim Thornton, and everyone else who has assisted us. We also owe a major debt of gratitude to the *Halifax Courier*, *Brighouse Echo*, *Todmorden News* and *Hebden Bridge Times*.

Finally, an enormous thank you to the Heritage Lottery Fund and the University of Huddersfield for supporting our work financially, and Sue Burnay at Sigma Books for all her help.

Peter Davies & Rob Light, 1 March 2006

Introduction

Between 2004 and 2006 we were fortunate enough to work on a unique £50,000 Project sponsored by the Heritage Lottery Fund and the University of Huddersfield: 'The Cricketing Heritage of Calderdale and Kirklees'. Our aim was to uncover and then reconstruct the history and heritage of local cricket in Halifax, Huddersfield, Dewsbury and District.

It was a stimulating task. We staged exhibitions in towns and villages throughout the area, created an interactive cricket heritage website, recorded the memories and reminiscences of local cricket folk, manufactured cricket history-related activity packs for schools, and established an e-archive as well as two traditional archives in Halifax and Huddersfield town libraries. We worked in partnership with local libraries and museums, West Yorkshire Archive Service, local cricket leagues and local cricket clubs. We were also assisted by a wonderful Project team - students from the University and many wholehearted volunteers whose motivation was simply passion and enthusiasm for the game and its history.

We were delighted when Sigma Books said they would be interested in publishing our research in a three-volume series of photographic histories, to make our work even more accessible to the local cricket community. In this trio of books our aim has been to reconstruct and represent local cricket history through the use of a variety of sources: photographs, documents, newspaper cuttings, maps, sketches, cartoons, and many other types of images and historical items. We hope you enjoy this book – and the series as a whole.

Calderdale is an area of West Yorkshire that centres on Halifax. The other major towns nearby are Todmorden and Hebden Bridge (to the west) and Brighouse and Elland (to the south and east). It borders on to Rochdale and Burnley on one side, and Bradford on the other. In the north it almost touches Keighley, in the south Huddersfield. Historically, it is an area of mills, factories and farming, though in recent decades it has diversified into financial services (the Halifax Building Society is world famous) and tourism (Hebden Bridge is a key centre and the local canal network has been restored to its former grandeur). It is also a very beautiful place – with spectacular views down the Calder Valley and at many other locations.

Cricket in the area now covered by Calderdale took off in the first decades of the nineteenth century. It appears that in June 1834 Halifax Clarence entertained Bradford on Skircoat Moor, and two years later Halifax Alliance crossed swords with Huddersfield Britannia. By August 1838, Todmorden CC had staged its first recorded match. In the 1860s inter-town matches were being organised involving Halifax, Elland and Brighouse. Smaller teams emerged, too. In 1870 a 'cricket battery' (an early 'bowling machine) was invented by Mr Swaine, a Halifax cricket professional, and in 1888 Halifax's Thrum Hall ground became a county venue. In 1887 the Halifax Parish Cup was established – and still today the Parish Cup final is a red letter day in the local sporting and social calendar. Calderdale has produced its share of England players (Bill Bowes and Peter Lever, for example) and also three grounds on which first-class cricket has been played (Halifax plus Elland and Todmorden). Cricketers who play in the Halifax League say the grounds are generally small. This may be true but they are also invariably attractive and charming.

We have split this book into 11 chapters. We start in Halifax and then head out – south and north, and then west through Sowerby Bridge and the Upper Calder Valley to Walsden and Todmorden, where Yorkshire meets Lancashire. Then we jump to the eastern fringes of Calderdale, and chapters 7, 8 and 9 introduce us to a variety of cricket communities on the Bradford side. We finish in the south, high up in the mountains, on the cusp of Kirklees and the M62.

The 11 geographically-themed chapters are designed to help the reader navigate the book and the story of cricket in the area as easily as possible. There are some minor overlaps, and it would have been possible to divide the area up another way if we had wished, but we had to settle on a structure, and we feel that the one we are using is helpful. The existing clubs in the area, and their history, are our main focus, but obviously, where appropriate, we make reference to a few of the several hundred former clubs we have encountered on our travels.

Here, we would also like to recommend the other two books in this series: Volume 2 – North Kirklees, and Volume 3 – South Kirklees. Together, the three books form a wonderful photographic history of cricket in this part of West Yorkshire. Please contact Sigma Books on 01635 281308 (sue@sigmabooks.fsnet.co.uk) or ourselves on 01484 472405 (p.j.davies@hud.ac.uk) if you would like to order them.

Our Project has taken us on a fascinating journey through local cricket history – the people and the places, the clubs and the leagues. And in a way, this series of three photographic histories enables us to re-live this amazing journey, and also to share it with you, the reader.

Peter Davies and Rob Light, 1 March 2006

Cricket clubs in Calderdale, 2006

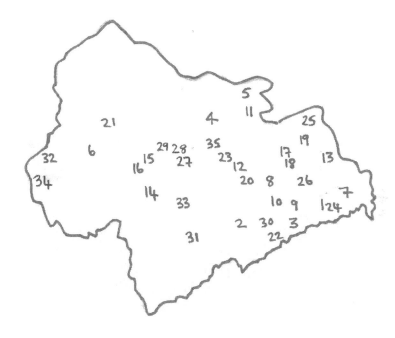

KEY

1. Badger Hill CC
2. Barkisland CC
3. Blackley CC
4. Booth CC
5. Bradshaw CC
6. Bridgeholme CC
7. Brighouse CC
8. Copley CC
9. Elland CC
10. Greetland CC
11. Illingworth CC
12. King Cross CC
13. Lightcliffe CC
14. Luddendenfoot CC
15. Mytholmroyd CC
16. Mytholmroyd Methodists CC / Halifax CC
17. Northowram Fields CC
18. Northowram Hedge Top CC
19. Norwood Green CC
20. Old Crossleyans CC
21. Old Town CC
22. Outlane CC
23. Queens Road Muslims CC
24. Rastrick CC
25. Shelf CC
26. Southowram CC
27. Sowerby Bridge CC
28. Sowerby Bridge Church Institute CC
29. Sowerby St. Peter's CC
30. Stainland CC
31. Stones CC
32. Todmorden CC
33. Triangle CC
34. Walsden CC
35. Warley CC

CHAPTER 1
URBAN HALIFAX: KING AND QUEENS

Thrum Hall, Halifax is one of three former county venues in the area of West Yorkshire covered by Calderdale and Kirklees (the others are Fartown, Huddersfield and the Savile Ground, Dewsbury). In the late nineteenth century, Yorkshire played three county games in Halifax – versus Gloucestershire in 1888, Middlesex in 1889 and Kent in 1897. The first dominant cricket club in Halifax was Halifax Clarence, probably named after King William VI, formerly Duke of Clarence before his coronation in 1830. Heir to Halifax Clarence CC was Halifax Trinity CC. Thrum Hall was home to the later Halifax CC; eventually this club folded and the ground was sold off. Today, a supermarket now stands where cricketers once plied their trade. King Cross CC is just as famous as the old Halifax CC, and many set-piece cricketing occasions were staged at their atmospheric ground, The Ramsdens. In the early twenty-first century, urban Halifax is also home to two clubs formed in the 1970s: Old Crossleyans, an old boys outfit who compete in the Halifax League, and Queen's Road Muslims, the superpower of the now-defunct Halifax Association who now have aspirations to join the Halifax League. Just outside the town centre lie Warley CC and Copley CC – two historic clubs who have enjoyed enormous success on the field in the last couple of decades.

Thrum Hall – former county ground, but now demolished.

A wartime club photo. 1944 was obviously a successful year for the Halifax club, with a Yorkshire Council title to show off.

King Cross CC in 1882, four years after formation. Note the array of garments and headgear on display. Stylised poses were also fashionable in this period.

OBJECT of the BAZAAR.

Fifty years ago the Club was formed, and play commenced on Skircoat Moor. From an enthusiastic Sunday School Team we have developed into a prominent eleven of the Yorkshire Council.

This progress in the game has brought with it larger financial responsibilities, for, although we are probably the only purely amateur team in the Council the great increase in the cost of ground maintenance wages, &c., together with the disappointing weather of recent summers, have caused our bank balance to be on the wrong side.

An urgent need for a tea pavilion, is also felt. We therefore appeal with every confidence to our friends to celebrate this Jubilee by coming to the Bazaar.

If you cannot come, then your gifts of money or goods will be gratefully acknowledged by,

In 1928 King Cross held a special bazaar to celebrate the 50th anniversary of the birth of King Cross Wesleyans CC. The club took the name King Cross in 1882.

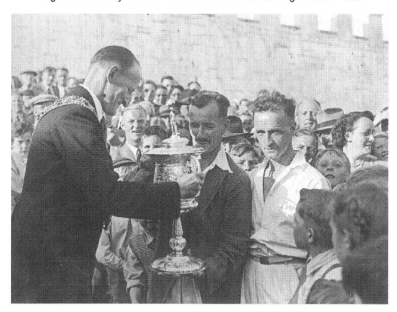

Captain Jim Bain receives the Parish Cup on King Cross's behalf in 1949.

3

**KING CROSS
CRICKET, BOWLING
and ATHLETIC CLUB**

The Ramsdens, Upper Kingston,
Hopwood Lane, Halifax

CENTENARY YEAR
1882 - 1982

50p

The club notched up its century in 1982 – and this special publication was produced to mark the occasion.

Queen's Road Muslims CC – winners of the Collinson Cup in 2003. The club was formed in 1974 by a group of young Asians who had grown up in and around Queen's Road in Halifax.

4

The *Halifax Courier* report on their 2003 triumph hinted at their frustrations playing in the Halifax Association. Since then they have expressed their desire to compete in the Halifax League.

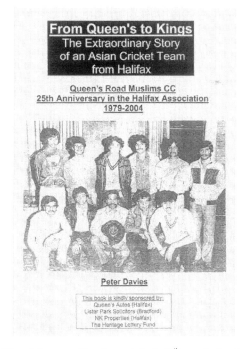

In 2004 a history of the club was written to mark their 25th year in the Association. A 1970s team line-up adorned the front cover of the booklet.

5

RAFA remember flying high

THE Halifax Association may be gone but many happy memories of playing in the league remain for at least one of its former clubs.

RAFA, members of the Association from 1952 to 1992, will mark the 25th anniversary of their last title success in 1980 with a reunion at Southowram Cricket Club on Sunday, May 15 (2.0).

Organiser Barry Chapman said 60 ex-club members and their families had already confirmed their attendance and he is hoping for double that number on the day. There will be a buffet tea for a nominal charge.

The idea for the reunion was instigated by Chapman, fellow former RAFA players Keith Walker and Eric Brierley and the club's ex-groundsman at Old Earth, Elland, Richard Haigh. They meet weekly for a pint and a chat and like other former Association players have been saddened by the league's demise this spring.

RAFA were Association champions five times and runners-up six times. They won the Collinson Cup in 1954 and were beaten finalists on five occasions.

The club left the Association for the Halifax League in 1983 but were voted out in 1989 and had three seasons in the Huddersfield Association before calling it a day.

They played at four grounds - Post Pitts at Ogden, Rolls Head, Spring Hall and Old Earth - and their former players include ex-Halifax Town player Tony Rhodes and Shay coaches Syd Farrimond and Brian Hendy plus former Halifax RLFC players Les Pearce and Owen Howard.

Chapman has managed to contact all but Lawrence Ramsbottom from the 1980 title-winning team and they will be joined at the reunion by four players from the 1952 team - Eric Felwell, Norman Riley, Ken Shield and Ken Windle.

Anyone wishing to attend the event can contact Chapman on (01422) 236653.

1980 champions: RAFA's line-up was, from the left, back row: Brian Kitchingham, Bob Kingdon, Bryan Stead, Lawrence Ramsbottom, Eric Brierley, Tony Rhodes and Gordon Wood. Front: John Bateman, Brian Rushworth, Brian Hendy (cpt), Syd Farrimond, Barry Chapman.

RAFA were a nomadic Halifax Association club.

This unidentified team won the Siddal Council Schools Cup in 1941.

West End CC – stalwarts of the Halifax Association – were based at the West End Hotel in Halifax.

Another Association team with a strong pub connection were New Riding CC who, with the demise of that competition, threw in their lot with Greetland CC.

Old Crossleyans is a relatively young cricket club, formed in 1976. It has a historic link with what is now the Crossley Heath School, located close by.

Star OCCC bowler and club secretary Paul Reynolds.

A 1st XI team photo from the 1980s.

EXTRAS!

Issue 1   February 1996

You've probably noticed all the snow outside which means that yet again the cricket season is upon us.

Welcome to the first edition of the 1996 Old Crossleyans Cricket Magazine **EXTRAS!**

Old Crossleyans are one of several local clubs who now publish their own regular newsletter.

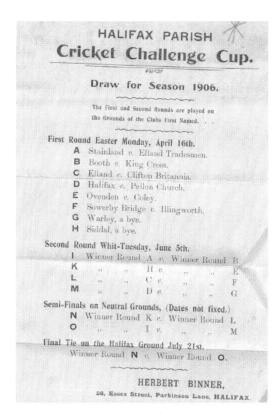

HALIFAX PARISH
Cricket Challenge Cup.

Draw for Season 1906.

The First and Second Rounds are played on
the Grounds of the Clubs First Named. . .

First Round Easter Monday, April 16th.
- A Stainland v. Elland Tradesmen.
- B Booth v. King Cross.
- C Elland v. Clifton Britannia.
- D Halifax v. Pellon Church.
- E Ovenden v. Coley.
- F Sowerby Bridge v. Illingworth.
- G Warley, a bye.
- H Siddal, a bye.

Second Round Whit-Tuesday, June 5th.
- I Winner Round A v. Winner Round B
- K   ,,   ,, H v.   ,,   ,,   E
- L   ,,   ,, C v.   ,,   ,,   F
- M   ,,   ,, D v.   ,,   ,,   G

Semi-Finals on Neutral Grounds, (Dates not fixed.)
- N Winner Round K v. Winner Round L
- O   ,,   ,, I v.   ,,   ,,   M

Final Tie on the Halifax Ground July 21st.
Winner Round **N** v. Winner Round **O.**

HERBERT BINNER,
58, Essex Street, Parkinson Lane, HALIFAX.

Warley is an old club, approximately a century old. They entered the Halifax Parish Cup in 1906 and received a bye through to the second round.

This is an early team photograph. We do not know the date, but we do know that the club had won a trophy/shield in this year. Note the proud-looking umpires and club officials.

9

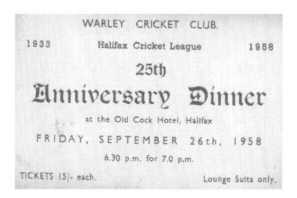

WARLEY CRICKET CLUB.

1933   Halifax Cricket League   1958

25th
Anniversary Dinner

at the Old Cock Hotel, Halifax

FRIDAY, SEPTEMBER 26th, 1958

6.30 p.m. for 7.0 p.m.

TICKETS 15/- each.   Lounge Suits only.

Warley CC was re-formed in 1933 after a period in hibernation. This dinner marked the 25th birthday of the 'new' club.

Dullaghan stars in Warley win

WARLEY Parish Cup hero Tony Dullaghan confessed he didn't expect to play a significant role in yesterday's final win over second division Southowram.

The off-spinner claimed seven for 81 and hit a vital 37 with the bat to secure his side a 79-run victory and help him pick up the man of the match award.

"Barkisland is not a ground I enjoy bowling on but I might have to change that view now," said Dullaghan who had hauls of 6 for 21 and 5-28 in previous rounds against Copley and Old Town respectively.

"I just concentrated on keeping things tight and got a little bit of turn occasionally. It just seemed to be my day and I really enjoyed it.

"When we discussed the game before hand it was always our intention for me to take the new ball and the plan worked better than I could have hoped."

Southowram, who beat two first division sides on the way to the final couldn't make it a hat-trick but skipper Mick Pollard, who led his side's fight with a half-century, was far from down-hearted.

"There were a couple of times in the match when I thought we were in with a real chance but it wasn't to be."

☐ CHAMPION ... Warley captain Andrew Oates lifts the Parish Cup trophy. PICTURES: Alan Barton.

Over the last couple of decades, Warley have scooped their fair share of silverware. This was the Parish Cup in 1992.

10

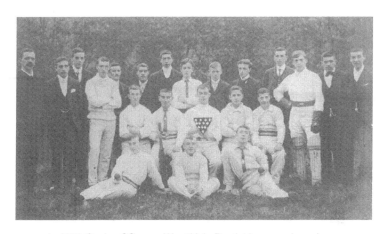

In 1901 Copley CC were West Vale Baptist League champions.

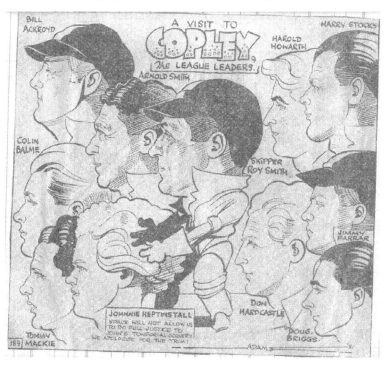

This 1951 *Halifax Courier* cartoon indicates that Copley were the team to beat in the immediate post-war years.

Club groundsmen watering the pitch in 1955.

This new club badge was designed in 1980. Copley's ground sits in the shadow of a giant railway viaduct – hence the image.

CHAPTER 2
ELLAND AND SURROUNDS: BRING ON THE AUSSIES!

Elland Cricket Club is one of the biggest in Calderdale. They play in the Huddersfield League and boast a rich history. Probably the most famous cricket match ever to take place in Calderdale was staged in 1878 at Elland's Hullen Edge ground, when '18 of Elland' took on the Australian tourists. The reputation of the club and the ground remains good, and in recent years the venue has hosted Yorkshire 2nd XI fixtures. Other cricket teams that once existed in the town include Elland Albert Mills, Elland Church Institute, Elland Edge, Elland Primitives, Elland St. Michael's, Elland Tradesmen, Elland Upper Edge, Elland Wesleyans, Elland White Star and Elland Y.M.C.A.. The two other clubs featured in this chapter are based in small nearby villages: Greetland CC (who have recently welcomed players from Greetland Village CC and New Riding CC) and Stainland CC, who both play in the Halifax League.

In 1878 '18 of Elland' took on the touring Australians – without doubt, the most famous match in the club's history. Above: A newspaper advert for the game. Below: The Australian team.

J. Blackham, F. Horan, G. H. Bailey, I. Conway, A. Bannerman, C. Bannerman, W. Murdock.
F. Spofforth, F. Allen, D. Gregory, (Capt.), T. Garrett, H. Boyle,
W. Midwinter.

The Elland Eighteen were: J. Lumb, H. Lockwood, B. Lister, N. Marsden, T. Foster, T. Walker, E. Osburn, W. Robinson, G. Hay, J. C. Pennington, H. Kaye, J. L. Byrom, The Rev. W. J. Kendle, T. Tong, R. Hudson, The Rev. E. A. Sandford, F. Shaw, W. Aspinall.

The Elland team for the prestigious 1878 encounter.

THE ELLAND CRICKET CLUB.—This club has arranged a capital programme for the coming cricket season. As will be seen from the list it has been decided to play most of the best clubs in this part of Yorkshire, and also to have a two days' encounter with the Parsees. The latter are an Indian cricket eleven which intend visiting this country this year, and in order to bring them up to a high state of perfection in batting, Henderson, the Surrey bowler, went out to India a few weeks ago purposely to give them some practice, before they start on their extensive tour. It has also been resolved to run two excursions this year instead of one as previously. The first eleven's fixtures are :—

Date.	Name of Club.	Where played.
April 24	Hodgson & Simpson's	Home.
,, 25	Upper Armley	Away.
,, 27	Brighouse	Home.
May 1	Holmfirth	Away.
,, 8	Manningham	Away.
,, 15	Low Moor	Away.
,, 22	Upper Armley	Home.
,, 29	Holmfirth	Home.
June 5	Heckmondwike	Away.
,, 7	Lockwood Tradesmen	Away.
,, 14	Rastrick	Home.
,, 15	Excursion to Blackpool	
,, 18	The Parsees	Home.
,, 19		Home.
,, 25	Rastrick	Away.
,, 29	Brighouse Butchers	Home.
July 3	Lockwood	Away.
,, 10	Halifax	Home.
,, 12	Lockwood Tradesmen	Home.
,, 17	Littleborough	Away.
,, 24	Lockwood	Home.
,, 27	Halifax Butchers	Home.
,, 31	Littleborough	Home.
Aug. 7	Manningham	Home.
,, 14	Halifax	Away.
,, 16	Excursion to Liverpool.	
,, 28	Low Moor	Home.
Sep. 4	Hodgson & Simpson's	Away.
,, 6	Meltham Mills	Home.
,, 11	Heckmondwike	Home.
,, 25	Brighouse	Away.

Denotes Day Matches.

The second eleven, besides playing most of the second elevens of the above clubs, contest with the following first elevens:—Salterhebble, Stainland, Dean Clough, Halifax Wesleyan, and Mr. J. F. Milner's Snowflake Rangers. The professionals this year will be Mr. J. Waterfall, of Derbyshire, and Mr. Joseph Waters, of Leeds.

OVENDEN UNITED CRICKET CLUB.—The following are the fixtures of the first eleven:—

Elland's fixture list for the 1886 season. Players would have headed east, west, north and south for fixtures in this period.

14

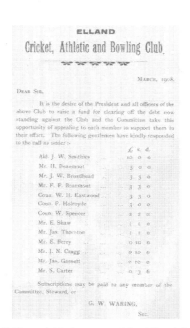

1908 – a debt-clearance crisis at the club.

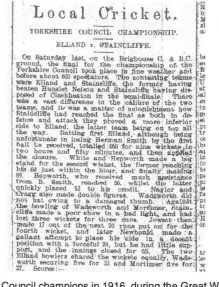

Elland were Yorkshire Council champions in 1916, during the Great War. This would have been a very important moment in their history.

A team photo from the 1930s. Officials outnumber players, which indicates the pride the club must have had in its on-field achievements (it looks like the club had won two separate competitions in this year). One of the trophies is the Byrom Shield, which means the date must be 1933, 1936 or 1939.

Star bowler Bill Dennis – third from the left – receives a gold watch after claiming his 1,000[th] Huddersfield League wicket in 1948.

Mrs. Crossland, Mrs. Sutcliffe (secretary), Mrs. Rawlinson (chairman),
Mrs. Sykes, (treasurer), Mrs. Berry

The club's Ladies Committee in 1960. This body would have been instrumental in fundraising and preparing matchday teas.

In 1977 Elland CC invited Ugandan dictator Idi Amin to open their new pavilion. In the end, the controversial invitation was withdrawn.

17

One of the early cricket teams in Greetland was called Greetland New Delight. This fixture came from 1862.

Greetland CC were Parish Cup winners in 1911.

1921 witnessed the opening of the new club pavilion.

Greetland CC officials and wives on the way to Pateley Bridge for a day out – some time in the 1920s.

Above: 'The Holme' – Greetland's HQ – probably in the 1920s.
Below: Club members working hard on ground maintenance.

Above left: Greetland bowler Willie Kershaw.
Above right: Two Greetland players celebrate a record stand or a significant match total.

1970 was 'Double' year for the club: the 1st XI won the Halifax League championship and the 2nd XI bagged the 1st Division title.

Staincliffe St. John's School : James Bush, Staincliffe, Dewsbury

Stainland : B. Mellor, Stainland

Stalybridge : Tom Hague, Park-road, Stalybridge. Pro. H. Hind, Notts

Stand : Wm. Chambers, The Elms, Whitefield. Pro. J. G.

An early mention of the Stainland club – 20 April 1886 in *Athletic News*.

Stainland.

√ 12.

This field is situate on a small occupation road leading from the Turnpike opposite the Duke of York Inn. It measures 110 x 80 yards, with a lair-crease 30 x 17 yards. There is a fair pavilion though small, but apparently no seating-accommodation.

The crease is laid conveniently so as to obtain more space for driving. The outfield is rough but fair on the whole. The crease is too small.

Above and below: Stainland's ground was inspected by the Halifax Parish Cup committee in the 1890s.

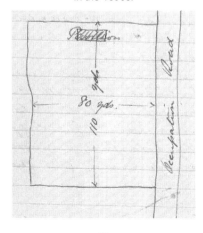

Expenses in Semi and Final Ties.

———•▶•◀•———

Stainland v. Luddenden Foot at Siddal.

Ground	...	...	1	0	0
Gatemen	...	...	0	2	0
Fares...	...	...	0	16	8
Umpires	...	..	0	5	2
Printing, &c....	...	...	0	7	9

2 11 7

Halifax Parish Cup documentation – 1901. Big-match occasions would have raised lots of money for the authorities.

STAINLAND WIN THE CUP.

Stainland won the Halifax Parish Challenge Cup on Saturday with comparative ease. Nelson batted first, and they made an exceedingly bad start, losing eight wickets for only 26 runs. Indeed, it looked as though the game would be over well within an hour, but at this stage the brothers Sunderland made a good stand. Harry, who had been in from the first, played carefully all through, but had no one to retain the opposite end until the appearance of his brother. These two took the score to 49 before Harry's leg stump was sent flying by Webster. The retiring batsman had 22 to his credit, whilst his brother came next with half that score.

There were four ducks on the Nelson side, due to the splendid bowling of Webster, whose average is well worth repeating. He bowled right through the innings and finished with the following record :—16 overs, 10 maidens, 6 wickets, 10 runs. Nelson were dismissed for 63.

On behalf of Stainland, Lister and Barker commenced operations, and, rather oddly, each scored 16, and then retired, the former being run out, and the latter falling a victim to a catch by Jagger, off Hartley. Binns (10 not out), Whitwam (12), and Furness (9, not out), with the assistance of four extras knocked off the score, and Stainland won by 7 wickets. They deserved their victory, for many have been the plucky fights they have made to get possession of the trophy. The result of Saturday's match is a fair criterion of the respective merits of the teams engaged.

Immediately the winning hit—a four—was made, there was a general rush to the pavilion, where the cup and medals were presented by the Mayor, Alderman W. Brear.

Stainland won the Parish Cup in 1901, 'with comparative ease'.

Stainland team photo – possibly 1922. A successful year.

This team photo dates from the 1940s or 1950s.

2nd XI team photo from 1968 – Stainland were Crossley Shield winners. Note the old clubhouse in the background.

The club's new pavilion was opened in 2001. This photo is taken from the bowling green side.

CHAPTER 3
BRADSHAW AND ILLINGWORTH: MILLS AND MINUTE BOOKS

Bradshaw and Illingworth are neighbouring communities to the north of Halifax and bordering on such places as Queensbury (another cricket village, but located within the boundaries of Bradford rather than Calderdale). The two clubs that are the focus of this chapter are historic rivals, but since Illingworth moved into the Airedale and Wharfedale League local-derby occasions have ceased – a matter of regret to some locals. Over the years, many players have turned out for both teams and there are still cricket-lovers in the area who maintain contact with both clubs.

HALIFAX PARISH

CRICKET CHALLENGE CUP.

Draw for Season 1891.

May 30th, 1891.

Elland Tradesmen v. St. George's......... A
Copley v. Ripponden................................. B

June 6th.

Siddal United v. All Souls' C
A   v. Triangle .... D
Illingworth St. Mary's v. Skircoat Green.. E
B   v. Ovenden Albion .... F
Lightcliffe v. St. John's Wesleyan .... G
Clark Bridge v. Police .... H
Dean Clough v. St. Thomas' I
Lord Nelson v. Greetland .... K
Salterhebble v. Bradshaw........................ L
Mountain v. Holy Trinity .... M

June 20th.

M   v.   C   .... N
King Cross v.   E   .... O
K   v. Elland .... P
G   v. Sowerby Bridge .... Q
I   v. Queensbury .... R
L   v. Halifax.. S
F   v. Hebden Bridge .... T
H   v.   D   .... U

July 4th.

O   v.   P   V
T   v.   N   .... W
S   v.   R   X
U   v.   Q   .... Y

July 18th.

Y   v.   V   .... AA
W   v   X   .... BB

The Bradshaw team that entered the 1891 Halifax Parish Cup was Bradshaw Mills CC.
They were drawn away to Salterhebble CC.

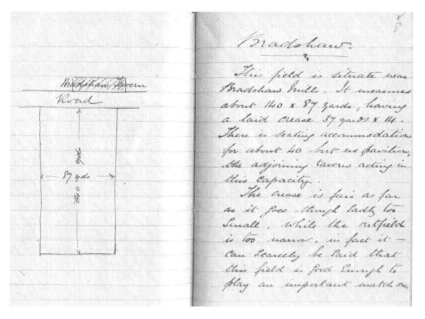

This Parish Cup ground inspection report from the 1890s tells us that the Mills ground had 'seating accommodation for about 40'.

The Bradshaw CC of today was founded in 1923. This team photo probably dates from the late 1920s.

L. WADDINGTON, JH HORNER, RH BARKER, NE CROSSLEY, R SUTCLIFFE, H HARTLEY, A HOPKINSON, DR KERSHAW, J WILSON,
W SHARP, A COLE, L SUTCLIFFE, W KING, JC THORPE, E INGHAM, J QUINN,
H SCALES, J BUTTERFIELD, L NORMINGTON, T BAMFORTH, W TWEEDY, A BATES.

This squad of players represented Bradshaw during the first summer of the Second World War – 1940.

In recent years Bradshaw have not been short of support at big-match occasions.

Their Bradshaw Lane ground has also witnessed its fair share of ground improvements.

[Handwritten minute book pages — St. Mary's Cricket Club, Illingworth 1884, listing President Revd. G. Oldacres, Vice-President Revd. F. L. Hughes, Treasurer Mr. I. Allison, Secretary Mr. Arthur Spencer, committee members and the club rules.]

These were the minutes of the first general meeting of the Illingworth St. Mary's club, held on church premises in February 1884. Point 2 says that individuals who wanted to play for the club must attend the church or Sunday school.

Savile Park. Score—Britannia 61, 66, and four or 60
KINGSTON v. WHITEGATE BLUE STAR.—On Monday. Score—Kingston 56 and four wickets to fall, Whitegate 22.
KINGSTON v. FOURTH FORM HIGHER BOARD SCHOOL.—Score—Kingston 71 and 103. Higher Board School 53 and 61.
ILLINGWORTH ST. MARY'S v. MOUNTAIN UNITED (2ND).—At Mountain. Score—Mountain 61, Illingworth 57.
OVENDEN ALBION v. SHIBDEN BLUE STAR —On the ground of the former. Score—Albion 7, Shibden Blue Star 43.
HALIFAX VICTORIA v. CATHERINE SLACK.—On the ground of the latter. Score—Victoria 48, Slack 13.
BOOTH TOWN METHODISTS v. AMBLER THORN —On the ground of the former. Score—Booth Town Methodists 74, Ambler Thorn 44.
ST. MARY'S 2ND v. LIGHTAZLES.—On the ground of the latter. Score—St. Mary's 50, Lightazles 15.
KING CROSS VICTORIA v. HALIFAX RANGERS.—On the ground of the former. An exciting finish resulted in a victory for the home team by three runs. Score—Victoria 29, Rangers 26.

This was the club's first ever fixture – away at Mountain United.

Yorkshire all-rounder Tom Emmett grew up in the village.

Illingworth won the Halifax Parish Cup in 1906. Church officials were well represented on the official club photo.

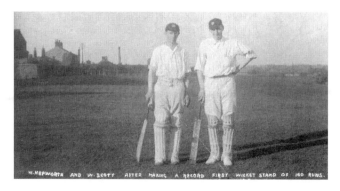

Club batsmen W. Hepworth and W. Scott took part in a record stand of 160, but the date this feat was achieved is unknown.

When Harry Hustwick died in 1960 he had amassed an incredible 76 years as a member of Illingworth St. Mary's C.C.. During this time the club, and local cricket in general, had undergone some remarkable changes and Harry was pivotal to most of them. His wonderful contribution to the club was first recognised by the presentation of a Rose Bowl to mark 60 years of involvement with Illingworth. When the new pavilion was opened in 1961, the year after Harry's death, it was fittingly named the Harry Hustwick Memorial Pavilion.

ILLINGWORTH St. MARY'S

(YORKSHIRE COUNCIL)

Cricket Club

MEMBER'S CARD   SEASON 1933

By 1933 Illingworth were rubbing shoulders with some very prestigious clubs in the Yorkshire Council.

Ladies Team of 1938 v. Gentlemen to mark the opening of the new Refreshment Hut.

Standing (L to R): Winnie Sykes, Clara E. Allen, Gladys Proctor, Norah Walker, Dorothy Northrop, Mary Briggs, Elsie Staff, Phyllis Pickles, Mary Campbell. Seated: Marjorie Moor, Marjorie Hirst, Ethel Morley, Mabel Hirst, Mary Campbell.

As in other parts of Halifax, Illingworth was a hot-bed of women's cricket during the 1930s.

In 1948 a group of Illingworth players featured in a *Halifax Green Final* cartoon.

Today, Illingworth are one of the few local sides to play in a regional league (the Airedale & Wharfedale). They also have a very smart website.

CHAPTER 4
SOWERBY BRIDGE: FLOODS, FIRES AND FINALS

Sowerby Bridge has a claim to be regarded as the 'cricket capital' of Calderdale. There are two clubs in the town, a third in nearby Sowerby village, and a fourth in Triangle, just down the road. Sowerby Bridge CC is located amid factories and fields on low land near the River Calder and the local canal. Sowerby Bridge Church Institute (SBCI) CC is situated high up in the valley, while Sowerby St. Peter's CC is a traditional village club with historic links to the St. Peter's church. Triangle CC is another valley-bottom club – famous for its picture-postcard ground and the little lad who earns a few pounds every Saturday fishing lost balls out of the nearby stream!

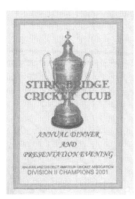
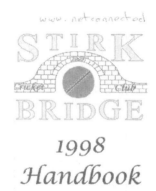

The young and the old. Above: The demise of the Halifax Association in 2005 meant that infant club Stirk Bridge CC – based at a pub of the same name in Sowerby Bridge – had to fold. Below: A report on an early cricket match in Sowerby Bridge in 1853. Note that by this time the Sowerby Bridge club had 50 members and was patronised by the local 'gentry and millowners'.

CRICKET MATCH.—We should not like to go back with Lord John Manners to the May-poles, monasteries, and Monkhood of the middle ages. However defective our social institutions still may be, we have made too much progress of late years to desire anything like a return to semi-barbarianism; but we do like to see, amidst all the talk about the culture of the moral and religious feelings, some attention paid to the education of the physical frame of the rising generation. The aristocratic students of Oxford, Cambridge, and Eton have donned their woollen jackets, and put their arms to the oar; gymnasia have sprung up in back gardens of every boarding school, and so cricket grounds are rising in all parts of the country wherever you meet with such a congregation of inhabitants as dare to call the place of their dwelling a town. The people are fond of the manly and health-promoting game, and it is pleasing to notice the interest which many of the class above "the people" take in it. The club at Sowerby Bridge, for example, which now numbers about 50 members, is well patronised by the gentry and millowners of the neighbourhood, and though comparatively in its infancy, is in a very flourishing condition. Last Tuesday, a match came off on their ground at Rose Hill, their opponents being eleven of the Mixenden Club. The severe Christmas weather having given place to a more seasonable atmosphere, there was a large concourse of spectators, and towards the afternoon many ladies graced the scene of contest with their presence. The players assembled about eleven o'clock, and shortly afterwards the game commenced, Sowerby Bridge going first to the wickets.

SOWERBY BRIDGE.

FIRST INNINGS.		SECOND INNINGS.	
J Horwood, b Wilson	1	b Varley	7
J Clegg, c Taylor, b Varley	5		
J Clegg, b Sutcliffe	0	not out	4
J Sorby (run out)	2	run out	0
J Sutcliffe (run out)	4	c Wilson b Varley	5
G. Highington, b Varley	10	b Sutcliffe	4
J. Ratcliffe (not out)	3	b Sutcliffe	5
C. W. Fielding, c Ambler, b Sutcliffe	10	b Sutcliffe	5
C. Schofield, c Simpson, c Varley	0	not out	11
Hartnett, c Shelton, b Nelson	1	b Nelson	22
J. Stobart (run out)	12	run out	3
Wides	13		8
Byes 1, Leg byes 1	5	Byes	2
	66		61

MIXENDEN.

FIRST INNINGS.	
T. Taylor, b Highington	11
W. Blackborough, c Clegg	11
N. Hoyle (run out)	0
J. Wilson, sen., (run out)	0
J. Wilson, jun., c Stobart, c Heighington	4
H. Sutcliffe, l b w, b ditto	0
J. Shelton, c Stobart, b Hartnett	12
H Simpson, b J. Sutcliffe	17
W. Ambler, b J. ditto	0
J. Friendley c J. Clegg, b Hartnett	2
J. Varley (not out)	0
Byes 8, Leg byes 2	5
	58

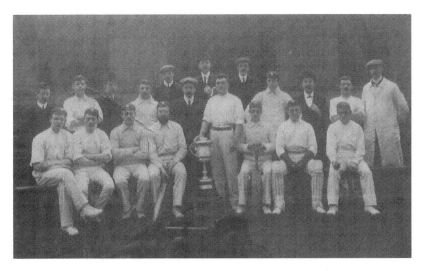

Sowerby Bridge CC in 1907 – proudly displaying the Parish Cup.

This 1921 cartoon implies that King Cross CC had come a cropper in an important match against Sowerby Bridge CC.

Halifax and Sowerby Bridge.

Cricket Clubs Win Championships.

Brilliant Victories.

RESULTS AT A GLANCE.

Halifax beat Whitwood Coll. by five wickets.
Bentley Coll. beat Illingworth by seven wkts.
Sowerby Bridge beat Salt's by six wickets.
Elland beat Linthwaite by three wickets.
Rastrick beat Almondbury by ten wickets.

Two championships were won by local cricket clubs on Saturday. Halifax beat Whitwood by five wickets to win the West Yorkshire League, while Sowerby Bridge secured an excellent victory over Salts, and thus made sure of the Bradford section of the Yorkshire Council.

1935 was a vintage year for two local clubs, including SBCC – winners of the Yorkshire Council's Bradford Section.

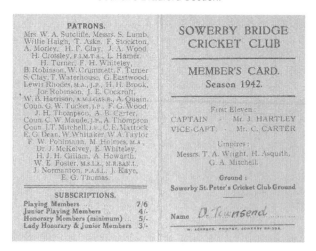

PATRONS.
Mrs. W. A. Sutcliffe, Messrs. S. Lumb, Willie Haigh, T. Asks, F. Stockton, A. Morley, H. F. Clay, J. A. Wood, H. Crossley, F.I.M.T.A., L. Hamer, H. Turner, F. H. Whiteley, B. Robinson, W. Crummett, F. Turner, S. Clay, T. Waterhouse, G. Eastwood, Lewis Rhodes, M.A., J.P., H. H. Brook, Joe Robinson, J. E. Cockroft, W. B. Harrison, A.M.I.GAS.E., A. Quain, Coun. G. W. Tucker, J.P., F. G. Wood, J. H. Thompson, A. B. Carter, Coun. C. W. Maude, J.P., A. Thompson, Coun. J.T. Mitchell, J.P., C. E. Mattock, E. G. Dean, W. Whitaker, W. A. Taylor, F. W. Pohlmann, M. Holmes, M.A., Dr J. McKelvey, E. Whiteley, H. J. H. Gillam, A. Howarth, W. E. Foster, M.S.I.A., M.R.SAN.I., J. Normanton, P.A.S.I., J. Kaye, E. G. Thomas.

SUBSCRIPTIONS.
Playing Members ... 7/6
Junior Playing Members ... 4/-
Honorary Members (minimum) ... 5/-
Lady Honorary & Junior Members 3/-

SOWERBY BRIDGE
CRICKET CLUB

MEMBER'S CARD.
Season 1942.

First Eleven :
CAPTAIN - Mr. J. HARTLEY
VICE-CAPT. - Mr. C. CARTER

Umpires :
Messrs. T. A. Wright, H. Asquith, G. A. Mitchell.

Ground :
Sowerby St. Peter's Cricket Club Ground

Name D. Townsend

During the Second World War, Sowerby Bridge CC had to lodge with Sowerby St. Peter's CC on account of their Walton Street ground being used by the government for military purposes.

In recent decades, Walton Street has suffered its fair share of natural disasters including flooding and fire.

SOWERBY BRIDGE.

THE COTE-HILL RESERVOIR. — On Wednesday evening a meeting of the waterworks committee of the local board was held at the Town-hall, Mr. Greenwood in the chair, there being also present Messrs. Shepherd, Wallis, Firth, and Garnet. It was resolved to sell the land at Hill Top, near Cote hill reservoir, and which is 300 square yards in extent, to Mr. John Shaw.

CHURCH INSTITUTE. — Up to Saturday last £5 had been subscribed towards the cricket club recently established in connection with this institute. The institute itself is in a promising condition, and numbers 50 or 60 members. The cricket club has taken a field at the Buck.

TEMPERANCE SOCIETY. —On Monday a meeting of this body was held in their room at Marsh fields; Mr. J. Sutcliffe presided, and addresses were given by Messrs. Jere Riley and J. Barnes. There was a good attendance.

THE FALL LANE ROAD. —To the Editor of the Ha'ifax Guardian. —Sir. —For a nice little job, see the manner our local authorities are repairing the steep gra-

This cutting from 1867 indicates that Sowerby Bridge Church Institute (SBCI) CC was formed in that year or just slightly earlier.

The calm before the storm: this team photograph was taken in the summer of 1939.

Above: 1964 Parish Cup semi-final. Below: SBCI win a tense final.

Surprise last-ball win by S.B.C.I. in final of Parish Cup

S.B.C.I., from Division Two of the Halifax Cricket League, pulled off a shock win over Booth at The Ramsdens on Saturday in one of the most exciting Parish Cup final finishes on record. With just one ball remaining, the scores were level.

The tension was tremendous, and all eyes were on Allan Hampshire as he faced the last delivery. He hit it for four and S.B.C.I. took the trophy for the first time since joining the Halifax League.

The 40-over system has certainly produced some thrilling cup cricket, and everyone present seemed to like the overs idea.

When the last over arrived, S.B.C.I. wanted five runs with one wicket remaining, but had only got four of them when the final ball arrived.

Half-century

Robert Tyas, top of the club's bowling and batting averages last season, gave another fine performance for S.B.C.I., for after taking two for 52 as opening bowler, he was undefeated with 45.

Hampshire had taken three for 59 and Albert Gawn was the side's top scorer with 57, his half-century coming in 31 minutes. Dennis Bowyer had two for 35.

Booth had two excellent per-formers in Willie Thomas and Neil Butterworth, and it was a pity that both had to finish on the losing side.

Thomas hit 92 in attractive style, including 16 fours (sixes are not allowed). His previous best scores in the league this year were 102 not out and 36.

Hat-trick

He needed eight runs off the last over to get his century, but from the first ball from Tyas, he was caught by Alan Jowett. His innings took 97 minutes and the side took 138 minutes for their 40 overs in rainy and windy conditions.

Butterworth did the hat-trick. With the last two balls of his first over, he captured the wickets of Geoff Storey and Bowyer with four runs on the board, and with the first ball of his second over he removed skipper Trevor Whitaker for a "duck" at the same score.

From collections taken during the match, Willie Thomas received £7 5s. 4d., Butterworth £5 10s. and Gawn £9 2s. The gate receipts totalled £23 7s. 6d.

The Mayor, Ald. D. Fawcett, J.P., presented the trophy. Details:

The details

Booth 167 for eight dec.—L. Patrick b Hampshire 3, F. Twemlow run out 10, K. Twemlow b Hampshire 16, D. Livesey c Gawn b Hampshire 0, W. Thomas c Jowett b Tyas 92, C. Radcliffe c Tyas b Bowyer 4, R. Midgley c Barlow b Bowyer 2, I. Riley b Tyas 28, D. Thomas not out 7, R. Walters not out 1, extras 4. Bowling: R. Tyas 17-1-52-2, A. Hampshire 13-2-59-3, D. Bowyer 9-0-35-2, T. Whitaker 1-0-17-0.

S.B.C.I. 171 for nine.—A. Sutcliffe b Walters 10, G. Storey b Butterworth 2, D. Bowyer c Radcliffe b Butterworth 0, T. Whitaker c Radcliffe b Butterworth 0, A. Gawn b Walters 57, R. Tyas not out 45, R. Turver c Livesey b W. Thomas 16, A. Jowett lbw b W. Thomas 7, G. Barlow b D. Thomas 15, T. Hinchcliffe b D. Thomas 3, A. Hampshire not out 9, extras 7. Bowling: D. Thomas 16-2-60-2, N. Butterworth 4-0-26-3, R. Walters 5-1-22-2, W. Thomas 15-0-56-2.

39

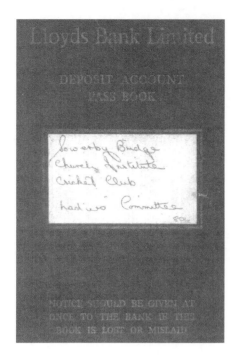

Like many clubs, SBCI once had a thriving Ladies Committee. This Ladies Committee cash book covered the years 1965-1975.

In 2003 SBCI members posed for a 'retro' team photograph – as if paying homage to their forebears at the club.

This is the earliest surviving team photograph of Sowerby St. Peter's CC – 1906. This picture now hangs in the club pavilion.

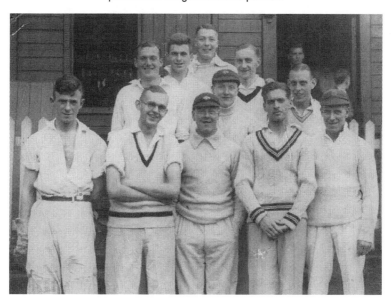

This team photograph comes from the 1930s – note the happy faces!

41

SOWERBY

Date	Name of Club	Gr'd.	Res
Apl. 15—Stainland	...	home	....
May 2—Dean Clough	...	away	....
„ 9—Triangle	...	home	....
„ 16—Cup Tie—Stones	home	....
„ 23—Booth	...	away	....
„ 30—Blakebroughs	...	away	....
Jun. 6—Mytholmroyd	...	home	....
„ 13—Barkisland	...	away	....
„ 20—Greetland	...	home	....
„ 27—Stones	...	home	....
July 4—Stainland	...	away	....
„ 11—Dean Clough	...	home	....
„ 18—Triangle	...	away	....
„ 25—Booth	...	home	....
Aug. 1—Blakebroughs	...	home	....
„ 8—			
„ 15—Mytholmroyd	...	away	....
„ 22—Barkisland	...	home	....
„ 29—Greetland	...	away	....
Sept. 5—Stones	...	away	....

SOWERBY BRIDGE

Date	Name of Club	Gr'd.	Res.
May 2—Siddal	...	home	....
„ 9—Halifax	...	away	....
„ 23—King Cross	...	home	....
„ 30—Salts (Saltaire)	home	....
Jun. 6—Chickenley	...	away	....
„ 13—Hartshead Moor	home	....
„ 20—Thackley	...	away	....
„ 27—Siddal	...	away	....
July 4—Illingworth	...	home	....
„ 11—Hartshead Moor	away	....
„ 18—Halifax	...	home	....
„ 25—Illingworth	...	away	....
Aug. 1—King Cross	...	away	....
„ 8—Gomersal	...	home	....
„ 22—Salts (Saltaire)	away	....
„ 29—Thackley	...	home	....

This fixture card comes from 1942 – when Sowerby and Sowerby Bridge were both playing at St. Peter's Avenue due to Walton Street (home of SBCC) being out of commission.

Donald Hoyle – skipper of this trophy-winning 1958 side – died only recently, and was an enormous help to us as we researched the history of his club.

The Triangle Reading Room Cricket Club.

It is gratifying to be able to state,that this truly national game is at length working its way into our own immediate neighbour-hood,with every promise of success.

Strange as such an assertion might sound to the ears of English-men in general,cricket is almost a new game here:but seeing its characteristics are a fine healthy and athletic exercise in the open air,we feel certain that it only needs to be known in order what it may be duly appreciated by the youth of this neighbourhood. here is most undoubtedly a vast moral good to be achieved by the more general introduction of this game,and partly for this reason: that it necessarily prevents any addiction to intoxication,because those who wish to excel must altogether eschew excess

We believe it to be in every way calculated to foster regular and steady habits.

The Triangle Cricket Club of which none can be members who are not also members of the Triangle Reading Room,has started under very favourable auspices.It seems that in addition to a few honorary members,there are also forty members,and these assembled for their first game on Wednesday the 23rd August in a field kindly offered to them for that purpose by W.H.Rawson Esq. of Mill House.It was a fine summer's evening and full of promise for the future of this young Cricket Club.

This is a transcription of an 1862 source that makes mention of the birth of Triangle CC. It is interesting that the new club was connected to the local Reading Room.

A Triangle team photo from 1896. The players would probably not have worn the ties they are seen wearing on the field of play.

Halifax Parish Cup winners in 1955 – a major achievement for a small village.

The Magnificent Seven – the Triangle club's trustees in 1962.

44

The club reached 100 not out in 1862 – and celebrated by producing a special souvenir brochure.

CRICKET
TRIANGLE
TRIUMPH

MAN OF THE MATCH . Steve Beck

In the last few decades, Triangle have been one of the most successful clubs in Halifax League circles. This report features their 1998 Parish Cup triumph.

CHAPTER 5
UPPER CALDER VALLEY: MARY AND METHODISTS

The Upper Calder Valley centres on Hebden Bridge and Mytholmroyd, two charming towns located by the River Calder and Rochdale Canal and close to beautiful countryside and historic places. Hebden Bridge and Mytholmroyd are situated on the valley floor, but Luddendenfoot, Booth and Wainstalls are high up in the clouds, and the character of the respective cricket clubs reflects this. In all possible senses, the Calder Valley is a gorgeous part of Calderdale.

CLARENCE'S CLOWN CRI KETRRS
F.
HEBDEN BRIDGE.

On Saturday last the "Top Hat" Clown Cricketers, under the superintendence of Mr. Clarence, of Leeds, paid their second visit to Hebden Bridge, when the weather was beautifully fine. The manner in which the clowns, by their merry antics, amused the spectators last year re-united in the gathering together of a fairly large assembly on Saturday, notwithstanding that there were other attractions which had commanded the attention of the public. Shortly after one o'clock the clowns, attired in grotesque costumes, and adorned in not a meagre variety of gay colours, were promenaded through the town in a "theatrical" conveyance, and caused much merriment by their popular remarks

Hebden Bridge Cricket Club is proud to present:

'CRICKSTOCK'
The Fifth Annual Cricket Festival

Programme

FREE
to make a donation

Left: In 1885 Hebden Bridge entertained a team of touring clowns. Right: In 2004 Salem Fields, home of HBCC, was hosting a special music festival.

Heptonstall village is next door to Hebden Bridge. This is Heptonstall Slack 1st XI c. 1950.

HEBDEN BRIDGE LEAGUE.

	Pld.	Won	Lost	Dro.	Pts
Mytholmroyd	17	12	2	3	27
Bircholiffe	18	12	6	0	24
*Heptonstall Slack	18	10	6	2	20
*Heptonstall Parish	16	7	8	1	17
*Cragg Vale	16	7	9	0	16
H.B. Liberal Club	16	7	8	1	15
St. James's	16	8	7	1	15
Old Town	18	7	11	0	14
Myd. St. Michael's	18	6	12	0	12
Mytholmroyd Wes.	18	6	12	0	12

* Heptonstall Slack and St. James's have had two points deducted for playing illegal men. The points have been given to Cragg Vale and Parish.

Mytholmroyd were flying high in the Hebden Bridge League in 1901. Note the preponderance of cricket clubs in the valley.

EXPENSES – Semi-Finals and Finals.

CLIFTON v. MYTHOLMROYD,
At Norwood Green.

	1915 £ s. d.	1914 £ s. d.
Umpires	0 5 10	0 6 8
Use of Field	0 15 0	0 5 0
Clifton Fares	0 5 0	0 2 3
Mytholmroyd Fares	1 2 0	0 10 0
	£2 7 10	£1 3 11

ILLINGWORTH v. STAINLAND.
At Sowerby Bridge.

	1915 £ s. d.	1914 £ s. d.
Umpires	0 5 4	0 7 8
Use of Field and Tickets	0 15 6	0 11 9
Illingworth Fares	0 9 0	0 15 0
Stainland Fares	0 10 0	0 6 0
	£1 19 10	£2 0 5

FINAL.
MYTHOLMROYD v. STAINLAND,
At Halifax.

	1915 £ s. d.	1914 £ s. d.
Umpires	0 5 0	0 5 2
Ground	2 2 0	2 2 0
Gate Men and Rolling Ground	0 10 0	0 13 6
Filling Cup	0 5 0	0 5 0
Mytholmroyd Fares	0 13 0	0 6 0
Stainland Fares	0 8 8	0 6 0
Printing and Postage	1 3 0	1 8 0
	£5 6 8	£5 5 8

In 1915 – during the first summer of the Great War - Mytholmroyd reached the final of the Halifax Parish Cup, staged at Thrum Hall, and came out on top. Note the expenses for 'Mytholmroyd Fares'.

MYTHOLMROYD CRICKET CLUB
1ST XI LEAGUE CHAMPIONS 1948

To commemorate the remarkable bowling performance
in the season when C Pugh and H Wilcock were joint
winners of the League Bowling Averages with identical
analyses:-
Wickets 71   Runs 475   Average 6·69

MYTHOLMROYD CRICKET CLUB
1st XI   Halifax League   Division 1 Champions   1954

More success followed in 1948 and 1954 – and latterly in 2005.

HALIFAX CRICKET LEAGUE
President - D. Normanton

Present

The Parish Cup Final

Sponsored by

Briggs Priestley Limited
Engravers & Signmakers

At Sowerby Bridge C.C. on Sunday, August 7th, 2005.
Wickets Pitched at 1.30pm

Mytholmroyd C.C.
v Copley C.C.

Umpires
R. Wilkinson, I. Sykes
Reserve - B. Tennyson

48

Mytholmroyd Methodists had an overt church link. This is an early team photo from 1910.

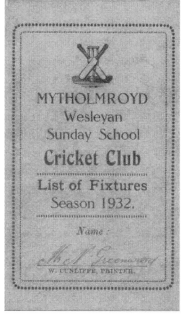

Above left: The club produced a special tribute to all members who had fallen during the Great War. Above right: The 1932 fixture card.

£90 in grants for new pavilion

GRANTS of £90 from the National Playing Fields Association were received last night by Mytholmroyd Methodist Cricket Club at the opening of a new pavilion which has cost £340. A cheque for £85 was received from the national association, and £5 from the West Riding association.

The pavilion was formerly a Sunday school classroom at the now closed Mount Zion Methodist Church, Mytholmroyd, and has been reconstructed, mainly by members and friends.

The opener, Mr. Cyril Thornber, of Mytholmroyd, congratulated the members on the excellence of the building, and the success they were having in the Halifax League this season.

Mr. Norman Greenwood, club chairman, who presided, spoke in appreciation of the hard work which had been put in to provide the building and the financial assistance which had been received. Mr. Thornber's family, he said, had been associated with the club for more than 60 years, as his father, the late Mr. Edgar Thornber, and uncle, the late Mr. Ralph Thornber were former players and members of the committee.

Mrs. F. Ayers, secretary of the West Riding Playing Fields Association, handed over the cheques for the grants to Mr. T. A. Foster, who was club secretary when the new pavilion scheme was started. Replying, Mr. Foster expressed thanks for the prompt way the association had dealt with the club's application.

Mr. Harold Whitehead, president of Halifax Cricket League, said he was proud that clubs which had been admitted during his presidency had shown enterprise and initiative in providing grounds and facilities of a high standard.

In a league game between the club and Mytholmroyd, the home side, batting first, scored 162 for no wicket. The match is being continued tonight.

Picture shows, left to right, Mr. Thornber, Mrs. Ayers, Mr. Whitehead, Mrs. K. Grace (chairman of the ladies' committee of the club) and Mr. N. Greenwood.

The club built a new pavilion in the early 1960s.

Right up to 2005 there was a lot of activity going on in the kitchen on matchdays. In the same year MMCC re-named themselves Halifax CC and are set to begin a new era in 2006 when they move into a new ground at Siddal, Halifax.

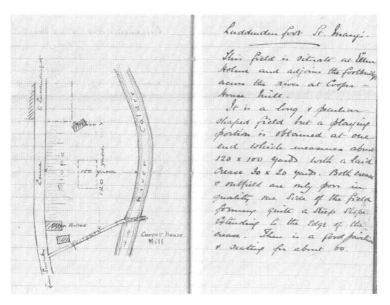

This Parish Cup ground inspection of Luddendenfoot St. Mary's ground dates from the 1890s. Even then there was 'seating for about 60'.

In 1894 Luddendenfoot CC were top of the tree in the Halifax Amateur League.

Luddendenfoot -v- Mytholmroyd – 1980 Calder Valley Cup 2nd Team Final

Front Row: M Sunderland, M Grimley, M Cockroft, B Charlesworth, D Oliver
Back Row: D Jackson, P Swain, S Lambert, D McCoubrie, G Turnbull, S Smith

This photograph currently hangs on the wall inside the club pavilion.

LUDDENDENFOOT
CRICKET CLUB

PRESENTS

LUDDENDENFOOT
CRICKET CLUB
PAST & PRESENT XI

V

CALDER VALLEY XI

OFFICIAL OPENING OF
PAVILION IMPROVEMENTS

SUNDAY 10TH AUGUST 1997
WICKETS PITCHED
2.00 P.M.

DONATION: £1.00
INCLUDING RAFFLE
PROGRAMME NO.

The club opened its new pavilion in 1997 – and secretary Sue Woolford was instrumental
in the successful application for grant money.

52

In 1927 Booth CC claimed the Halifax League title.

And in 1948 they bagged the Parish Cup.

In the 1950s Booth were a well supported club.

This special plate was designed in 1993 to help commemorate the BCC centenary.

In recent years the club has started to produce a special information booklet each summer.

Webster's CC used to play at Cross Roads, Wainstalls – as can be seen from these fixture cards.

WAINSTALLS CRICKET CLUB

1950 - 2000

GOLDEN JUBILEE

Left: Wainstalls CC celebrated their 50th Anniversary in 2000. They had moved into the Cross Roads ground, but the club went out of business with the demise of the Halifax Association in 2005. Right: WCC had always encouraged women's and junior cricket.

55

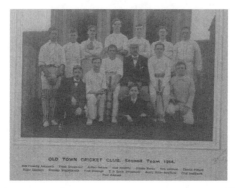

One of the earliest surviving photos at Old Town CC – the 2nd XI in 1914.

In 1948 Old Town bagged the Hebden Bridge League & Cup 'Double'.

Club members toiling hard on the new ground at Boston Hill, 1956.

Above and below: The Boston Hill ground was officially opened on 8 June 1957.

NEW GROUND AFTER THREE YEARS' WORK

Old Town Cricket Club's 'dream came true'

'ONE OF THE FINEST VOLUNTARY EFFORTS'

WHEN Lord Treigarne of Cleddau opened the Old Town Cricket Club's self-made new ground at Boston Hill, Hebden Bridge, on Saturday, rain cut short the ceremony.

But the heavy downpour failed to damp the spirits of those who had looked forward to the official opening as marking the fulfilment of what the club president, Mr. Raymond Ashworth, described as "a dream come true."

Lord Treigarne, who was presenting the National Playing Fields Association, gave the heartening

club although the children's sports were called off.

A vote of thanks was proposed and seconded by Messrs. John N. Butterworth and Roy Greenwood, and a bouquet was presented to Lady Treigarne by Leslie Blackburn the small daughter of one of the club members.

Three-year task completed

It was in January, 1954, that a piece of ground was bought for £685 by Old Town Cricket Club from Hepton Rural Council at Boston Hill, Wadsworth. It showed contained a circular pond, a huge rockery, and was surrounded by trees. The N.P.F.A. granted £390, and the West Riding Association allocated a grant of £35. One hundred and thirty trees around

The club 2nd XI in 1995.

CHAPTER 6
TODMORDEN & DISTRICT: LANCASHIRE HOTPOT

There is a part of Calderdale that looks towards Lancashire - Rochdale and Burnley – rather than Halifax. Walsden, the club situated closest to the county border, play in the Central Lancashire League, while Todmorden, their near neighbours, compete in the world-famous Lancashire League. Add in Bridgeholme CC of the Halifax League – situated on the road from Todmorden to Hebden Bridge - and you have a trio of clubs all playing in different competitions. Between 1893 and 1959 there was a Todmorden League, which featured such teams as Cornholme, York Street, Todmorden White Rose, Eastwood, Cross Stone, Lumbutts, Castle Street, Harley Wood, British Picker, Knotts, Walsden St. Peters, Patmos, Inchfield Bottom, Roomfield, Todmorden Church, Cloughfoot, Bridge Street, Unitarians, Wellington Road and Lane Bottom.

The Todmorden CC rules of 1839.

An early Todmorden line-up from 1869. Note the amazing and flamboyant clothes!

An 1864 painting of the Centre Vale ground.

Centre Vale, Todmorden, staged this prestigious fixture in 1874.

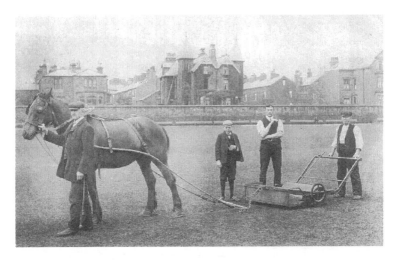

Rolling the wicket 1908-style.

A local newspaper cartoonist focused on the Todmorden club's cricketers in 1933.

A new scorebox was opened at Todmorden in 1939.

This Todmorden team photo dates from 1981. Pakistani Test star Mohsin Khan is second from the right on the front row; Brian Heywood, co-author of the excellent history of TCC, *Cloth Caps and Cricket Crazy*, is sat far right on the front row.

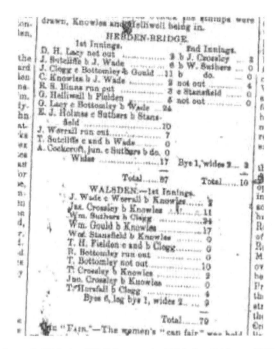

An early Walsden CC fixture against Hebden Bridge – 1863.

A Walsden team photo from 1920. The men in suits may be umpires or club officials.

Two undated – and very contrasting – views of Scott Street, home of Walsden CC.

Frank Scott – a legend on and off the field at Walsden CC.

One of Walsden's traditional local derbies in the Central Lancashire League is against Littleborough. Here the characters involved in yesteryear are brought to life by a local newspaper cartoonist.

Hebden Bridge Cricket League Winners

Bridgeholme Cricket Club, champions of the first division of the Hebden Bridge Cricket League, and winners of the knock-out competition. Back row: Coun. H. Cockcroft (chairman of committee), J. Horsfall, D. Hollinrake, B. Hartley, A. Martin, J. Kaye, J. Greenwood, R. Ashinson, T. Mitchell (scorer). Front row: Miss M. Sutcliffe (secretary), A. Leeder, R. Greenwood, W. Davies, L. Davies, J. Duffield, Mr P. Sowden, J.P. (president).

Bridgeholme CC was formed in 1950. This team photo comes from 1953.

In 1991 Bridgeholme scooped the Collinson Cup – this was the triumphant team line-up.

The Bridgeholme club has a sense of humour too. This was a fancy dress party staged at the club pavilion which featured cricketers and friends.

Station House – Bridgeholme's roadside ground – is extremely picturesque.

Club stalwart Keith Hudson built the new scorebox at the venue.

TIMES AND GAZETTE, FRIDAY, SEPTEMBER 12, 1952

Eastwood's First Cricket Team

The reconstruction and drainage of the old East-wood cricket field now taking place has revived many recollections of the past glories of the old club. We print above a photograph of the first Eastwood cricket team, which dates back over 50 years. The members of the team were: Left to right, standing: D. Crossley (secretary), L. Netherwood, G. Heys, T. Oldfield, A. Fielden. R. Sutcliffe. Seated: S. Sowden, J. Mitchell., T. H. Walton, F. Speak, T. Speak and J. Fielden.

Bridgeholme CC is situated in an area called Eastwood. This photo is of the extinct Eastwood CC c.1902.

67

CHAPTER 7
TOWARDS BRADFORD: LIGHTCLIFFE, NORWOOD GREEN AND SHELF

Communities in the east of Calderdale tend to look towards Bradford, and the three clubs featured in this chapter all play, or have played, in Bradford-based leagues. Lightcliffe play in the world-famous Bradford League – in fact they perceive their club to be the only truly 'rural' club in a predominantly 'urban' competition. Meantime, Norwood Green and Shelf have spent much of their life in the Bradford Central League.

William Ackroyd, who donated the picturesque Wakefield Road ground to Lightcliffe Cricket Club around 1875.

A Lightcliffe team photo from around 1890. Note the flamboyant clothes being worn and the array of headwear. Often this would denote the socio-economic background of the players.

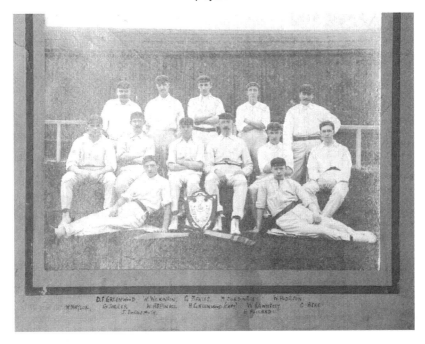

This was the group of players that claimed the Halifax Parish League title in 1905.

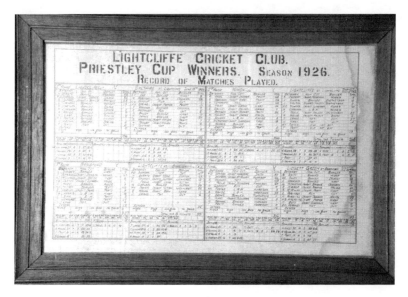

In the year of the General Strike – 1926 – Lightcliffe scooped the Priestley Cup. They had joined the Bradford League only two years earlier. This board now hangs in the club pavilion as a reminder.

Herbert Aspinall played his first game for Lightcliffe in 1940 and went on to star a remarkable 501 times between then and 1967. Aspinall is remembered for much more than just his playing skills; he was also a long serving secretary and League rep.. He was also groundsman for the last 20 years of his life.

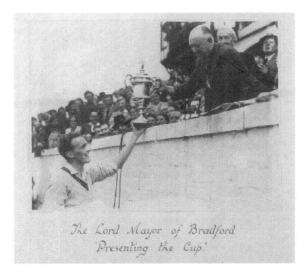

The presentation of the Priestley Cup to the Lightcliffe side in 1950.

Lightcliffe Cricket Club

Pavilion Extension

In 2002 the club announced plans to redevelop their quaint red pavilion.

LEAGUE TABLES.
FIRST DIVISION.
FIRST TEAMS.

	P.	W.	L.	D.	Pts
Norwood Green	18	14	1	3	31
Siddal	18	8	2	8	24
Stainland	18	10	4	4	24
Sowerby Bridge	18	7	6	5	19
Greetland	18	7	7	4	18
Triangle	18	5	8	5	15
Clifton Britannia	18	4	8	6	14
Ovenden	18	4	10	4	12
Elland Edge	18	3	9	6	12
Mytholmroyd	18	4	11	3	11

SECOND TEAMS.

Siddal	18	14	3	1	29
Triangle	18	11	4	3	25
Ovenden	18	11	5	2	24
Sowerby Bridge	18	10	5	3	23
Greetland	18	8	7	3	19
Stainland	18	7	9	2	16
Mytholmroyd	18	4	10	4	12
Clifton Britannia	18	5	11	2	12
Elland Edge	18	4	11	3	11
Norwood Green	18	4	13	1	9

In 1911 Norwood Green bagged the Halifax & District League 1st XI title...but came bottom of the 2nd XI table.

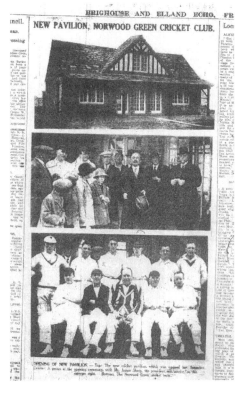

In 1930 the club unveiled a new pavilion building.

The pavilion today – it is one of the most attractive in the area.

A happy-looking Norwood Green line-up from 1975.

Norwood Green stalwart Keith Barker is seated in the middle of the front row in this 1988 team picture. The 2nd XI had just claimed the Bradford Central League championship.

In 1997 Norwood Green lifted the Thrippleton Cup.

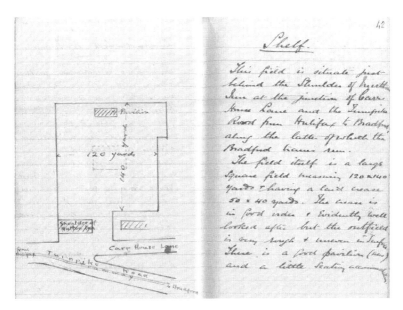

In the 1890s Shelf CC were subject to a Halifax Parish Cup ground inspection. The Shoulder of Mutton pub – mentioned on the second line – is still the local landmark.

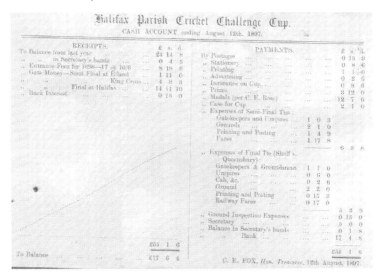

Shelf carried off the Halifax Parish Cup in 1897. This balance sheet details the cost of cup final day.

In 1903 Shelf were the first-ever winners of the Bradford League.

for Queensbury, Thornton reaching a total of 40 against Queensbury 96 (Chatburn 30, Bartle 28, Proctor 20).

Shelf Clough Mills were soundly beaten by Wibsey. The latter club knocked up 110, getting rid of Clough Mills for 45.

Todmorden (137 for five wickets) gained their second victory in their match with Colne 105.

King Cross struggled hard to win at Mirfield in their

Another team were also playing in Shelf in 1903.

Yorkshire and England legend Len Hutton visited Shelf CC in 1950.

Neil Firth leads the Shelf team out during the 1962 season.

Winners of the Thrippleton Cup in 1972.

The old pavilion building at Shelf's ground. It has since been replaced by a more modern facility.

In 2003 the club staged a special Centenary Dinner. This brochure – full of archive photos and memories – was published to accompany the occasion.

CHAPTER 8
NORTHOWRAM AND SOUTHOWRAM: FROM CHOIRBOYS TO THE CARIBBEAN

The communities of Northowram and Southowram are linked historically – as can be guessed from their similar-sounding names. Today, Northowram is famous for its hospital and its two cricket clubs – whose grounds are adjoining. Southowram is a village renowned for its quarries and its intriguing cricketing history. Once there were several clubs in the village; then they all folded; and then a 'new' club emerged in the 1970s.

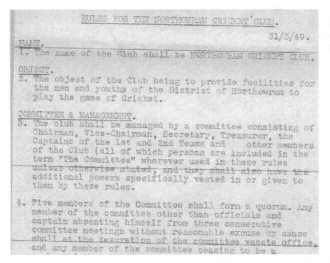

In 1920 Northowram Parish Cricket Club – later Northowram CC and Northowram Fields CC - staged a special fundraising dance.

The rules of the newly-formed Northowram club in 1949. Note Point 2: the aim of the club is to serve 'men and youths' in the local area.

The old Northowram CC pavilion in 1989.

During the following year fire ripped through the building.

In 1998 the newly-merged club – Northowram had joined forces with Fields CC from Bradford - celebrated the 50th Anniversary of Bradford Central League Cricket at Westercroft Lane with a special fixture.

An early Northowram Wesleyans side. This photo was taken in 1921, two years after the club had been formed. The club later became known as Northowram Hedge Top CC.

Another early team photo: note the smartly-dressed club women in the background.

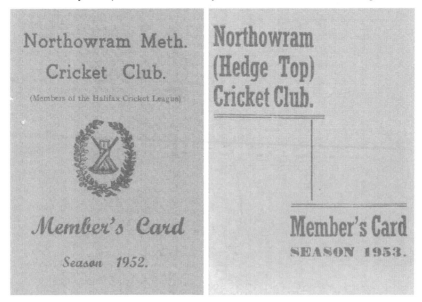

Northowram Meth.
Cricket Club.
(Members of the Halifax Cricket League)

Member's Card

Season 1952.

Northowram
(Hedge Top)
Cricket Club.

Member's Card
SEASON 1953.

Two membership cards from the early 1950s. The name change occurred prior to the 1953 season.

Spectators at the Hedge Top Lane ground.

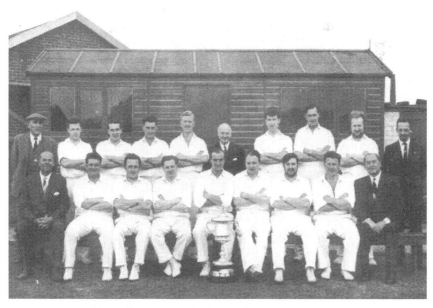

Hedge Top were Halifax Parish Cup winners in 1965.

Horse stops play!

Working on the square.

Building the practice nets.

Northowram is a rugby league stronghold – and the Hedge Top club have strong links with the Bradford Bulls.

The Hedge Top club have also travelled to the Caribbean.

LIGHTCLIFFE v. DEAN CLOUGH MILLS.—Played at Hopwood Lane, Halifax. Scores:—*Dean Clough Mills*—Mitchell 0, Fielding 12, Cahill 1, Chapman 1, Crowther 3, Hodgson 29, Sutcliffe 10, Crossley 0, Hogg 0, Nettleton 3, Patterson 1, extra 1, total 59. *Lightcliffe*—Wood 0, Smithson 3, Ingham 7, Torvell 1, Field 1, Dawson 4, Nettleton 1, Ferguson 4, Lloyd 2, Harrison 0, Naylor 0, extra 1, total 24.

ST. ANNE'S CHURCH CHOIR, SOUTHOWRAM v. PELLON-LANE VICTORIA.—Played at Southowram last Saturday, and resulted in an easy victory for the home eleven. Score:—Southowram, 27; Pellon-lane, 7. Noble and Goodyear bowled well, the former taking five wickets for three runs and the latter three wickets for the same number of runs. Farrar (pro.) was unable to play with the home eleven. Southowram score:—J. W. Cockroft 3, W. Cockroft 1, Malkin 1, Goodyear 3, Noble 1, Rawlinson 2, Fawthrope 5, Sanderson 4, Jowett 3, Clayton 2, Beaumont 1, extra 1, total 27.

HOVE EDGE v. RANGE BANK.—At Swales Moor. The visitors won by three runs after a very even game. Allen and Oates bowled well for Hove Edge, the former taking 6 wickets for 11 runs, the latter 4 for 9 runs. Scores:—*Range Bank*—Milner 0, Haigh 4, Tankard 4, Brearley 1, Whiteley 4, Crossley 1, Balratow 0, Crossley 1, Bottomley (not out) 5, Bennet 0, Crowther 0, total 20. *Hove Edge*—Oates 2, Turner 6, Marsden 4, Smith 0, Dennison 1, Allen 0, Hepworth 1, Rawnsley 6, Tiffany 2, Sykes 1, Hodgson (not out) 0, total 23.

BRIDGE END ("A" team) v. RASTRICK ROVERS.—At Woodhouse. Scores:—*Bridge End*—J. Lancaster 4, Wood 2, E. Rawlinson 0, H. Bottomley 0, Shaw 0, Rushworth 4, W. Bottomley 6, Webster 0, Fox 4, Southworth 9, Owen 0, extra 1, total 23. *Rovers*—G. Thackray 1, J. Waddington 2, Rayner 1, Cardwell 4, Bentley 2, Brook 0, Clarke 4, Jagger 2, Parker 2, Murgatroyd 1, Halham 0, extras 2, total 21.

Our Wedding Rings are made of pure Gold,
And whosoever wears them will have love untold.

An 1889 reference to St. Anne's Church Choirboys CC (Southowram).

SOUTHOWRAM ST. ANNE'S.

As the result of the bazaar held last October the above club is in a good financial position. Already something like £40 has been spent in the purchase of a new tent, roller, nets and other necessary cricketing material. The members, who have promise of a successful season, opened on Saturday with the usual members' match. Sides were chosen by Mr. Carnelley and Mr. Raynor (captain and vice-captain), and the match ended in a win for Mr. Carnelley's team by 12 runs, after an exciting finish, the scores being 54 and 42. After the match the players, at the invitation of Mr. Carnelley, had tea together at the Pack Horse Hotel. When the cloth was cleared Mr. S. Addy took the chair, and at his request Mr. Carnelley (this year's captain) had the pleasure of presenting Mr. T. Noble (last year's captain), who has recently been married, with a handsome copper kettle, mounted on a brass stand. Mr. Noble suitably replied, thanking the members for their kind wishes and very handsome present, also for their support last season, and promised his best efforts and services towards the club's success in the coming season. The remainder of the evening was spent in a social manner, most of the members contributing songs, etc.

Season preview – 1896.

BRIGHOUSE CRICKET LEAGUE.

RESULTS UP TO DATE.

	P	W	L	D	P
Primitive Methodist	14	10	2	2	22
Bridge End Congregational	14	6	2	6	18
Hove Edge	14	6	3	5	17
Clifton Britannia	13	6	4	3	15
Park Church	14	5	5	4	14
Southowram St. Anne's	12	4	5	3	11
Parish Church	14	3	10	1	7
Rastrick Church	13	1	10	2	4

The club competed in the Brighouse Cricket League – this was 1898.

The Southowram St. Anne's club also plied its trade in the Halifax and District Church League – this cutting is from 1910.

A team photo from the late 1970s – soon after the 'new' Southowram CC had been founded.

1982 – the scene at Ashday Lane after tipping had taken place. This would be the Southowram club's new ground.

The Southowram 2nd XI in 1982.

In 1992 Southowram were Halifax League 2nd Division champions.

Sky's the limit after Rams gain big break

FLEDGLING club Southowram were soaring up in the clouds last night after landing their first major trophy success.

The Ashday Lane outfit, only formed in 1978, winged in for a 13-run victory over Outlane in the Halifax Parish Cup final at Copley.

In a game which mirrored the sides' Section A clash at the end of May, slight favourites Southowram adopted catch-us-if-you-can tactics, posting a big score and then just having enough in the bowling department to hold off Outlane's fightback.

Fiaz Haider did not let down

ِ Ian Rushworth

his growing army of admirers with a polished 68 on a prime batting track.

But the game's real damage was done in the last four overs of the Southowram innings when Jake Smith and Ben Harvey transformed what looked likely to be a good total into a very useful one with 49 extra runs.

Outlane started their reply brightly, but their way and were then hit back into contention by Aurang Zeb and Sohail Rana only to finally run out of batsmen with seven balls left.

In front of a 700-strong crowd on a loud, breezy day,

Southowram's Richard Eastaugh won the toss and elected to bat.

Haider and Phil Vout made lightning progress to 37 for none off five overs.

Dean Swift bowled too short and was soon hit out of the attack but Southowram, 60 without loss after 10 overs, lost some momentum as Jeremy Calahan and Andrew Gregory tightened their length and line.

The diminutive Haider lost Vout, trapped leg before to left-arm medium pacer Gregory, with the total on 72 but went on to reach his half-century in the 19th over.

Haider and Zahid Mahmood added 80 for the second wicket but Rana gave Outlane a much-needed boost with two wickets in three balls.

Haider looked to have set his stall out for a century but was trapped leg before and

skipper Eastaugh had his off stump clipped.

Mahmood's innings had flourished but, after reaching 57 with a six through the railway arches, he fell to a slick piece of stumping from Gary Shuttleworth.

That brought ex-Outlane skipper Smith and Harvey together at 181 for four and the powerfully-built pair upped the scales firmly their side's way with some awesome hitting in the closing stages.

The final over, from Zeb, went for 13 with Smith smashing two sixes and Harvey one before the latter, a Bradford Belle Academy player, was caught at long off from the penultimate ball of the innings.

Those who wrote off Outlane at tea were having second thoughts as Glyn Croft and Shuttleworth scored 51 off the first 10 overs.

Both then perished in successive overs, Croft hitting a rare full toss from Tariq Mahmood to Chris Jagger at mid-off and Shuttleworth, who had some fine drives in his 26 being bowled by a full-length delivery from Smith.

John Pettinger was ruled caught behind without troubling the scorers and against Outlane still the total on 107 when Dave Beaumont was adjudged stumped by David O'Shea off Smith.

Left-armers Tariq and Smith kept things tight and when they completed their 10-over stints, Outlane were half-way to their target with 17 overs left and six wickets in hand.

An ultra-defensive field offered Outlane some easy runs but Mel Wilks still couldn't resist the temptation to go for a big hit and he skied the ball to

Tariq at long-off.

Zeb was slowly picking up the pace and after he had reached 32, Andrew Selachere was unlucky to see the inspired Smith nonchalantly snap up his straight drive in the deep — an act which clinched his man of the match award.

Swift made a quick exit but Zeb found a willing partner in Rana and they reduced the requirement to 38 runs off the last four overs.

When Jagger bowled Zeb for 60 it looked all over but Sohail had other ideas, hitting a four and two sixes later in the over to leave 21 required off three.

It was not to be. Zahid Mahmood, who generates plenty of pace off three strides, bowled Rana and Jagger conducted the last rights by shattering Calahan's stumps to clinch Southowram's moment of glory.

They scooped the Parish Cup for the first time in 2000.

90

CHAPTER 9
BRIGHOUSE AND RASTRICK: OLD GIRLS AND OLD BOYS

Brighouse and Rastrick are famous for their brass band – and also three historic cricket clubs. Brighouse CC play in the Bradford League and now possess an exquisite, state-of-the-art ground. Today, Rastrick boasts two clubs, located very close to each other. Rastrick CC currently play in the Huddersfield League, while near neighbours Badger Hill CC – formerly Rastrick New Road CC – compete in the Huddersfield Central League.

This book is one of the most amazing cricketing artefacts that has survived to the present day. It is entitled 'Brighouse CC & BC Records 1873-1933', and it contains handwritten reports and scorecards from the club's early years.

This letter (to Todmorden CC, trying to arrange a fixture in 1878) indicates what a high-profile and prestigious club Brighouse was. Note the distinguished letterhead

In the last summer of peace before the Great War, Brighouse CC hosted a special workshops competition, with local works teams fighting it out for supremacy on the pitch.

Grand CRICKET MATCHES

ON THE CLIFTON ROAD GROUND,

THIS EVENING (JUNE 19th) AT 7 O'CLOCK. LADIES' MATCH.—
TECHNICAL SCHOOL GIRLS v. NEW ROAD GIRLS.

Admission: Adults 2d., Boys and Girls, 1d.

SATURDAY AFTERNOON (JUNE 20th) AT 2.30 p.m.
BRADFORD LEAGUE MATCH. BRIGHOUSE 2nd v. BINGLEY 2nd.

Admission: Adults 2d., Boys and Girls, 1d.

WEDNESDAY EVENING (JUNE 24th) AT 7 O'CLOCK. LADIES' MATCH.—
CARR GREEN GIRLS v. HOVE EDGE GIRLS.

Admission: Adults 2d., Boys and Girls, 1d.
Roll up to watch the fair sex use the willow.

In the 1930s women's cricket was all the rage in Brighouse and surrounding towns. This advert from the *Brighouse & Elland Echo* shows how games were publicised.

92

This was Brighouse Central School Old Girls cricket team in the 1930s.

Brighouse were Bradford League champions in 1960. Club skipper Geoff Hirst is sitting in the middle of the front row.

The pavilion at the old Clifton Road ground.

The Brighouse club's new state-of-the-art ground. They moved in at the start of the 2004 season.

94

DALTON V. RASTRICK.

This match was played at Rastrick, on Saturday last. The Rastrick had the choice of innings, and went first to the wickets, and were disposed of for 45 runs. The Dalton scored 57, thus winning the match by 12 runs. The ground was not in good condition, which accounts for the small scoring. Score:—

RASTRICK.

W. Swaine, b A. Sykes	6
J. Bromley, run out	5
J. Thornton, b A. Sykes	7
W. Ramsden, c Challenger b Sykes	4
J. Earnshaw, b Ramsden	3
J. Holmes, l b w, b Bradley	3
C. Turner, b A. Sykes	0
G. Rushforth, b A. Sykes	7
J. Mayall, c Hall b Sunderland	2
A. Jordan, b A. Sykes	0
K. Mayhall, not out	0
Extras	8
Total	45

DALTON.

D. Shaw, run out	3
C. Challenger, b Jordan	0
J. Crossland, b Jordan	0
C. H. Bradley, c and b Swaine	33
A. Sykes, b Mayhall	0
J. E. Eastwood, c Mayhall b Jordan	4
T. Hall, c Ramsden b Jordan	2
T. Ramsden, b Mayhall	1
K. Mellor, not out	1
R. Nelson, c Holmes b Swaine	0
W. Sunderland, c Earnshaw b Swaine	2
Extras	0
Total	57

One of Rastrick's earliest recorded games came in 1868, when they entertained the famous Dalton team from Huddersfield. The report says that the 'ground was not in good condition'!

Brighouse v Rastrick 2nd at Brighouse Saturday June 14th 1873

RASTRICK 2nd		Brighouse N.A.	
J. Marshall b Broadley	19	R. Lister not out	1
J. Hill c Lister b Simms	2	S. Day c Dowkes b Hinchcliffe	1
H. Brearley b Broadley	13	J. Pilling b Hinchcliffe	2
W. Shillitoe run out	2	H. Simms b Hinchcliffe	0
G. Dowkes run out	3	W. Gill not out	8
O. Gibson b Simms	1	Extras	5
J. Sutcliffe b Simms	0	for 3 wkts Total	17
J. Hinchcliffe c Crossley b Simms	0		
A. Redfearn b Simms	0	DRAWN OWING	
J. Shillitoe not out	0	TO	
H. Hinchcliffe b Ellis	2	RAIN	
Extras	13	DRAW	
Total	55		

They played local rivals Brighouse in 1873 but the weather had the last word.

The club was known formally as Rastrick United in the early period. This piece of correspondence dates from 1878.

Rastrick's HQ at Round Hill is renowned for its distinguishing local landmark. This photograph was taken on 18 April 1953 – the first day of the cricket season.

Rastrick CC – 15 May 1954. Note the black arm bands. Maybe a player or official or spectator at the club had died during the previous week.

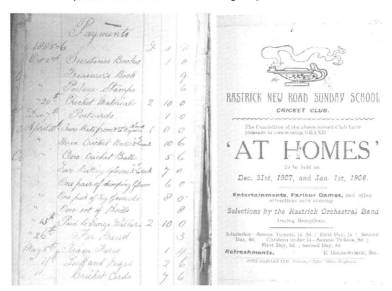

Left: Badger Hill CC used to be known as Rastrick New Road CC and were linked to the local church. The earliest date we have for the early club is 1885-6 (a payments book).
Right: In 1907-8 the club were putting on entertainment for local people.

Rastrick New Road CC in 1921 – winners of the Huddersfield Cricket Association League Lumb Cup. The stylised poses were common in this era.

In 1929 the club were doing their bit for local charity.

Rastrick were winners of four trophies in 1937. There are 15 club officials in this photo and 22 cricketers (maybe the full 1st XI and 2nd XI).

The decade is the 1950s and the bowler here is the legendary 'Chucker' Peel.

End of the road

ONE of the most famous names in Huddersfield cricket will soon be disappearing.

Rastrick New Road are to become Badger Hill Cricket Club when a new 20-year lease, negotiated with ground owners Yorkshire Thornhill Estate, begins at the end of next month.

They are amicably severing their links with the local Sunday school in order, says committee member Trevor Bottomley, that "we can play Sunday cricket."

"The trustees of the Sunday school have given us permission in the past to play the Lumb Cup and Crosland Trophy finals on Sundays if we got there but

By ROBERT GLEDHILL

we had to play the previous rounds on Monday and Tuesday evenings," explained Mr Bottomley, a stalwart of the Huddersfield Association's oldest club.

"At the end of November, the lease runs out so we thought it a good time to break away from the Sunday school and start up under a new name. The trustees of the Sunday school have allowed us to keep the equipment and the cash—most, of which, has been raised by the players—that we had, although if the club folds in the first five years then all the assets will

revert to the Sunday school."

There seems little danger of that as there is evidence of Rastrick New Road having existed over 125 years ago, although actual records date back to 1896, when they first played at Badger Hill.

During their history, the New Roaders have captured the Section "A" title 22 times and the Lumb Cup on 18 occassions. They were also beaten finalists against Edgerton this year.

Huddersfield Association match and registration secretary Barry Allison has confirmed that the club will keep their Section "A" status under their new name.

In 1987 the club broke with the local church and reinvented itself as Badger Hill CC.

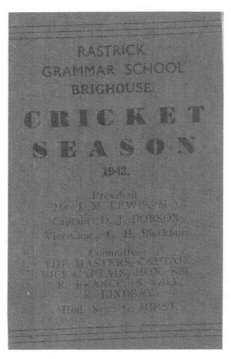

RASTRICK
GRAMMAR SCHOOL
BRIGHOUSE.

CRICKET
SEASON
1942.

President
Mr. J. M. LEWIS, M.A.
Captain: D. J. DOBSON
Vice-Capt.: G. H. Blackburn

Committee:
THE MASTERS, CAPTAIN,
VICE-CAPTAIN, HON. SEC.,
R. FRANCE, S. GILL,
R. LINDSAY.
Hon. Sec.: L. HIRST.

Two other interesting cricket clubs in the area. One side attached to a school (above) and another connected with a church (below).

Memory Will Play Again

Lane Head Church Cricket Club: Brighouse
1967-2003

John Brooke
Kelvin Lawton
Club Records by Andrew Hadden

100

CHAPTER 10
RYBURN: BARKISLAND AND STONES

Once upon a time there were a handful of cricket clubs in the Ryburn and Ripponden area. Now there are just two: Barkisland CC – ambitious and aspirational in the Huddersfield League; and Stones CC – whose Swift Cross home is one of the most striking and spectacular cricketing locations in the whole of Calderdale.

Barkisland made their Halifax Parish Cup debut in 1938. This page from the official minute book says they were knocked out in the second round.

BARKISLAND WIN PARISH CUP FOR FIRST TIME

Emphatic victory over Illingworth

Beating Illingworth by five wickets at the Ramsdens on Saturday, Barkisland won the Parish Cup for the first time. Batting first, Barkisland moved comfortably towards a score of 151 for five when their innings was suspended. The only hope the Illingworth attack raised was just before the century mark when two quick wickets suggested a possible break-through, but Barkisland quickly covered up.

A. Holroyd contributed a sound 51 by the type of batting which the occasion demanded. In reply, Illingworth were never out of trouble. None for one, two for two, 14 for three told a pathetic story. Wilson Smith with a gallant 39 tried hard to stabilise the situation, but never found a seconder. G. Ellis, five for 48, was the course of the downfall, and strangely enough he seldom bowls for Barkisland.

After the game the trophy was presented to the Barkisland captain J. Maude, by the Mayor, Ald. F. Sharp, J.P. Mr. S. Stott and Mr. F. Berry spoke on behalf of the contesting clubs. Gate receipts

Long-service player's good form

A polished half century by Hartley, plus another good contribution by Woodcock and useful scores from Aspinall, Booth and Hirst enabled Lightcliffe to compile a good score at Saltaire. The home team were out for 50, Mallinson taking six for 19 in 9.6 overs and Clarke lent fine support, taking four for 30 in 10 overs and taking three catches off his colleague's bowling.

Lightcliffe have re-engaged Albert Hartley for seasons 1951 and 1952. Hartley, a left-arm bowler and right-hand batsman, began his professional career with the club in 1925. For Lightcliffe he has dismissed 680 batsmen for 881 runs to average 16.18, and

R. Sunderland st Jackson b Naylor 23, H. Palmer lbw b Naylor 43, Proctor b Naylor 5, B. Sutcliffe lbw b Hunt 15, O. Smith b Hunt 7, E. Illingworth c Walton b Briggs 3, G. Brooks b Briggs 3, T. Sunderland b Briggs 6, N. Tatham not out 2, extras 6.
Water Haigh 144 for six.—T. Gill b Illingworth 34, B. Edwards c Brooks b T. Sunderland 3, B. Walton c Brooks b Sunderland 12, A. Briggs c Palmer b Sunderland 21, D. Clazebrooke b Brearley 13, A. Houghton not out 23, A. Fox run out 2, J. Hunt not out 10, extras 6.
Second teams: Sowerby Bridge 87, Laisterdyke 88; Tong Park 137, King Cross 83 (R. Scott seven for 20).

Sykes Cup final

ELLAND v. LINTHWAITE
(at Fartown, Huddersfield)
Elland 131 for three innings suspended.—T. Thornton b Swan 51, W. L. Drinkwater lbw b Swan 23, G. Askew not out 31, F. R. Sykes not out 5, extras 9.
Linthwaite 152 for eight.— P. Pearson c Askew b Drinkwater 31, P. Garside st Kettlewell b Drinkwater 15, G. Place c Drinkwater b Holroyd 3, R. Bower b Drinkwater 8, R. Brook lbw b Judge 11, B. Chappell lbw b Farrar 30, C. Beaumont c Sykes b Askew 12, K. Oldham st Kettlewell b Drinkwater 18, E. W. Jebson not out 15, H. Kenworthy not out 0, extras 7.

Bradford League

In 1950 they won the trophy for the first time.

This team won the Halifax League title in 1956.

In 1957 three pairs of brothers turned out in the same Barkisland team: Schofields, Hallowells and Tennysons.

Australian Test legend Dennis Lillee opened the new Barkisland pavilion in 1975.

When they netted the Halifax Parish Cup in 1981 they became the most prolific club in the competition's history.

Barry Tennyson was a successful Barkisland captain and wicketkeeper. He is now Chairman of the Halifax Cricket League.

BARKISLAND

V

Hall Bower

Saturday 24th April 2004
Wickets Pitched 1.30PM

Today's Match Day Sponsor is:

See Back Page and Contact Peter for Great Peugeot Deals

Ground Admittance £1.50p
Child/OAP £0.75p

The club produces a colourful and glossy programme for each of its encounters in the Huddersfield League.

The club is indebted to its hardworking tea ladies for their weekend efforts.

105

The cricketers of Stones posed for this photograph after winning the Halifax League in the 1920s.

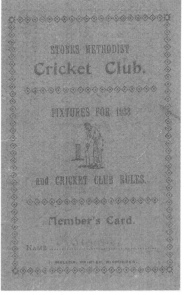

Some time between 1921 and 1938 the club changed its name from 'Wesleyan' to 'Methodist'.

Above and below: Stones CC were Parish Cup winners in 1938.

The Mayor (Ald. F. Watkinson, J.P.), presenting the Cup to the Stones C.C. captain, at "The Ramsdens," on Saturday last.

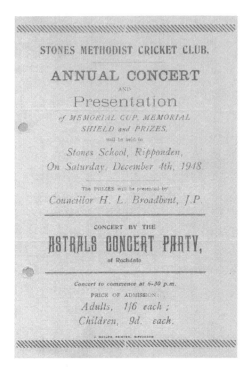

This is how the club celebrated the 1948 cricket season.

The club won the Parish Cup again in 1954.

— STONES CRICKET CLUB —

Opening of the New PAVILION

STONES C.C.
versus
THE PRESIDENTS ELEVEN
SUNDAY 22 AUGUST 1971

Wickets Pitched at 2.30 p.m.

Tickets 5p
Refreshments Available

A new pavilion building was opened at Swift Cross in 1971.

Club officials and the pavilion in 1995 — after another phase of redevelopment had taken place.

Blackley and Outlane could lay claim to being the two cricket clubs in Britain situated closest to a motorway. The Blackley ground lies adjacent to Junction 24 of the M62, while Outlane's home patch sits only yards away from cars zooming to and from Leeds and Manchester. Naturally, therefore, both clubs have had to endure motorway-related difficulties and problems. Today, the Halifax League is home to BCC and OCC, though both have also competed in the Huddersfield Association. The clubs are near neighbours, and from high up at Outlane's ground you can spot Blackley in mid-distance – a truly spectacular view, with Halifax, Elland and the rest of Calderdale forming the backdrop.

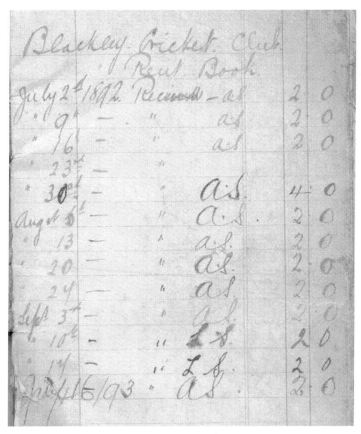

A Blackley CC rent book from the 1890s.

The earliest surviving photograph of Blackley's Lindley Road ground.

Blackley's pavilion in 1910.

A Blackley team photo from about 1910 – note the two umpires (far left and far right) in their long white coats.

A trophy-winning team from the pre-1914 era.

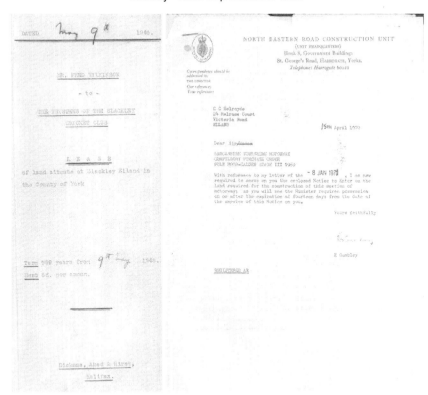

Blackley - Lumb Cup winners in 1936.

Ground lease – 1946. Motorway problems – 1970.

Blackley C.C.
~~severs~~ link
of sixty years

Record balance of £109

"We have a record balance in hand of over £100, and for a village club this is a great feat, especially when we hear of local clubs in danger of closing down," said the secretary, Mr. E. Ambler, at Thursday's annual meeting of Blackley Cricket Club.

Mr. Ambler said that the 1953 season had been notable because the first team had lost only two matches, both to Almondbury, and they had come near to winning the Huddersfield Cricket Association championship for the first time.

Referring to the club's decision to join the Halifax League next season, Mr. Ambler said that this would sever a 60 years link with Huddersfield cricket. He hoped they would be able to prove them-

Blackley left the Huddersfield Association in 1954.

Lindley Road two years later in 1956.

114

The hardworking groundsmen – undated.

The view of Blackley's ground from the boundary fence at Outlane's HQ.

The Swinging Sixties: above – a club annual dinner; below – women cricketers from the Blackley club.

General Meeting

April 28/19. Chairman Mr Ed. Boothroyd
No present 11

This meeting was held to arrange or
decide, when we should take over, full
control of the field.
He had an interesting account, from Mr
Coun. Pilling, of the interviews he had,
with Mr Coun. Robson on the question of
taking the Cricket Field for allotments.
He gave a brief history of how the field
was broken up for the purpose of food
production

It was passed that we take hold of
the field at the end of this year 1919

Passed that the Sec: write the Trustees
of the U. M. F. Church asking permission
to change the name of the Cricket Club,
from. U. M. F. Church Cricket Club to
that of Outlane Cricket Club and
the Trustees to renounce all claim on the Club.

One of the first Outlane CC meetings after the First World War.

The old Outlane pavilion – removed from Cote Farm and erected at Lindley Moor.

OUTLANE'S SUCCESS

Almondbury Wes. Beaten in Vital Game

Outlane became champions of the Association on Saturday when they beat Almondbury Wesleyan at Outlane by the big margin of 101 runs. The position before the match was that the winning side also won the championship. In the case of a draw there would have been a tie between the two clubs and Blackley.

The Outlane batsmen showed championship form, and made a total of 151. The chief contributors were R. Pearson (40), R. Hargreaves (22), R. Blackburn (22), C. Heap (19), and E. Lumb (18). Almondbury failed badly, and made only 50. H. Crawshaw, who scored 19, was the only player to reach double figures. Outlane's principal bowlers were J. W. Dyson, who captured six for 16, and E. Lumb, who had three for 11.

Outlane ... ... 151 Almondbury Wes. ... 50
Y.M.C.A. ... ... 94 Cowcliffe Church ... 51
(Each side had only ten men.)

SECOND ELEVENS

Almondbury W. ... 54 Outlane (for 6 d.) 157
Cowcliffe Church Britannia Works
(for 5) ... ... 47 for 7 dec.) ... 154
Rowley H. (for 5) 46 D.B.S. Ath. Club... 43

FINAL LEAGUE TABLES.

First Elevens.

	P.	W.	L.	D.	Pts.
Outlane	18	9	1	8	24
Blackley	16	10	3	3	23
Almondbury Wes.	16	8	2	6	22
Brit. Dyestuffs Cor., Ltd.	18	9	4	3	21
Rowley Hill	18	9	4	3	21
Rastrick New Road	18	7	8	1	15
Birchencliffe Church	16	4	7	5	13
Britannia Works	16	5	8	3	13
Cowcliffe Church	16	4	10	2	10
Y.M.C.A.	16	3	9	4	10
D.B.S. Athletic Club	16	1	15	2	4

Second Elevens.

	P.	W.	L.	D.	Pts
Outlane	18	13	1	2	28
Rastrick New Road	18	12	1	3	27
Cowcliffe Church	16	8	4	4	20
Birchencliffe Church ...	18	6	6	4	16
Almondbury Wesleyan ..	16	5	6	5	15
Blackley	18	6	8	2	14
R. D. C., Ltd.	18	5	7	4	14
Britannia Works	16	4	9	3	11
D. B. S. Athletic Club	18	3	11	2	8
Rowley Hill	18	2	12	2	6

BOWLING

J. M. Dyson, Outlane (v. Almonndbury Wesleyan) ... ... 6 for 16
— Stancliffe, Cowcliffe Church (v. Y.M.C.A.) ... ... 5 for 20

In 1932 the club's 1st XI and 2nd XI both claimed Huddersfield Association titles.

Outlane CC – 29 May 1950.

Outlane - Lumb Cup winners in 1954.

Minister's help may be sought to solve motorway plan deadlock

Sports clubs face disruption

MR. DENIS HOWELL, M.P., the Minister of Sport, is to be written to by the Huddersfield Sports Advisory Council in an effort to hasten a solution to the procedural deadlock which is confronting some local sporting organisations affected by the Lancashire—Yorkshire Motorway proposals.

One of the town's keenest cricketing enthusiasts, Cllr. Herbert Robinson, a member of the Town Council and vice-president of the Huddersfield and District Cricket League, is prepared to go to see the Minister himself if it will help matters.

The organisations concerned are the Outlane Golf Club and Outlane Cricket Club. The Outlane-Calder section of the Motorway scheme, work on

claim, is dreadfully slow and this places them in a most difficult position to plan and negotiate for alternative site accommodation.

Huddersfield Corporation were approached by the Sports Advisory Council in February asking if they had any alternative land available for the cricket club, who would lose their field.

The Parks Committee discussed the matter, and decided that there would be no objection to the use of an area of land at Pool Fields as a cricket field.

When a question was raised in the Council Chamber at the April meeting, the reply given was that the cricket club were "very happy" with that decision.

The club suffered serious and potentially fatal M62-related problems in 1968.

Treble winners – 1975.

CENTENARY YEAR
1897 — 1997

Outlane CC notched their first century in 1997.

INDEX